FABULISM

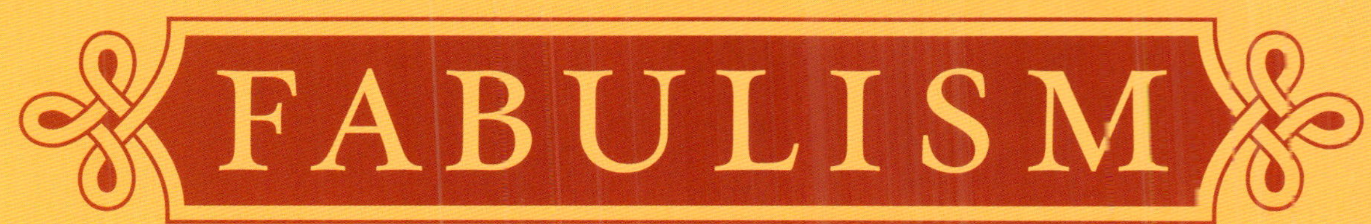

CARROLL DUNHAM

ELLEN GALLAGHER

CHRIS OFILI

NEO RAUCH

MATTHEW RITCHIE

KLAUS KERTESS

January 31–April 25, 2004

JOSLYN ART MUSEUM Omaha, Nebraska

LIBRARY OF CONGRESS CATALOGING-IN-PUBLICATION DATA

Kertess, Klaus.

Fabulism : Joslyn Art Museum, Omaha, Nebraska January 31–April 25, 2004 / Klaus Kertess.

p. cm.

ISBN 0-936364-33-5

1. Fantastic, The, in art—Exhibitions. 2. Painting, American—21st century—Exhibitions.

I. Joslyn Art Museum. II. Title.

ND1460.F35K47 2004

753′.7′0973074782254—dc22

2003021677

DESIGNED BY THOMAS WHITRIDGE

& PRODUCED UNDER THE SUPERVISION OF INK, INC., NEW YORK.

TYPESET IN REQUIEM.

1500 COPIES PRINTED IN CHINA.

CONTENTS

FOREWORD

A YEAR AGO Joslyn Art Museum engaged the services and expertise of art curator and critic Klaus Kertess to advance the Museum's reinvigorated contemporary art program. In addition to his highly regarded experience and knowledge in the arena of contemporary art, Kertess has brought to Joslyn a new sense of awareness and discovery, tempered by a personal sensitivity, that one might expect from a New Yorker assessing the ambitions of a Midwestern museum.

In addition to advising Joslyn on new directions and acquisitions in its contemporary art focus, Kertess has been charged with organizing innovative exhibitions on a regular basis. This, the first group show created by Kertess for this endeavor, brings together five international painters under the intriguing title of *Fabulism*. These artists share a propensity to explore, within the exigencies of their own individual style and time, highly imaginative paths in the direction of fantasy, mythology, and allegory, drawing upon the traditions of the romantics and symbolists of the nineteenth century, the surrealists of the early twentieth century, and the heroic pictorial statements of the abstract expressionists at mid twentieth century. In this exhibition Kertess has presented us with some fascinating stepping stones which link the recent past to the present, bringing us along for the discovery, encouraging us to partake of the evocations of five remarkable artists who, while vastly different painters, share the gift of myth-making.

Fabulism is the first step in what we anticipate will be a very exciting program of exhibitions from Klaus Kertess over the next several years.

J. BROOKS JOYNER
Director

BRUSHES WITH GODS, DEVILS, DEMONS, MONSTERS, THE MILKY WAY, AND PLANCK'S CONSTANT

IN THE LAST DECADE, growing numbers of artists, in various mediums, have set sail for the further shores of fantasy to once more explore and reinvent myth, allegory, and fable. Not since the psychovisual excesses of Surrealism, as well as those of subsequent individual forebears, including Philip Guston, Peter Saul, and Sigmar Polke, have we been confronted with such fanciful protagonists and iconographic complexity. This exhibition focuses on five of the most noteworthy of these geographers of the imagination: the painters Carroll Dunham, Ellen Gallagher, Chris Ofili, Neo Rauch, and Matthew Ritchie. Unlike the Surrealists, these five neither explore under a single flag nor adhere to a common manifesto, but rather create within the panoply of multiplicity endemic to the contemporary art world. Their individual influences range from scientific theory to Mayan glyphs to hip hop music, to name but a few; and their paintings range from schematic painterliness to lavish icons reveling in craftlike decorativeness and procedures. Nonetheless, common themes and aims exist within this group and can be seen in the exhibition. This essay points to some of the links that loosely join these artists.

The late modernism practiced in the 1960s and 1970s continued to expand the self-containment and visible clarity of the procedures of art making initiated by Manet and Cézanne in the late nineteenth century. How to paint remained the paramount concern. The 1980s witnessed the breakdown of and reaction against modernism's historical imperative and ushered in a free-for-all of ...*isms,* all jostling for position under the umbrella of post modernism (as in post historical). Anything was possible. Modernism became but one of many alternatives; its uniqueness became moot. Sherrie Levine could create a photographic duplicate of a Walker Evans photograph and call it a Sherrie Levine. Gerhard Richter's simultaneous desires to paint like Caspar David Friedrich and to create abstract paintings cued by Jackson Pollock proved more laudable than schizophrenic. What to paint began to acquire some urgency. Quasi-documentary narratives sometimes not averse to agitprop and driven by issues of race, gender, and sexuality claimed increasing space on museum walls and floors by the early 1990s, as new gender-neutral words claimed their place in our vocabulary.

At the same time, numerous artists, also interested in narrative and also anxious to capitalize on the freedoms presented by the collapse of modernism's hegemony, sought to plumb the depths of the vagaries of the everyday world, be they racial, sexual, or scientific, through the invention of imaginary worlds. What to paint now was enfolded in myth, fable, and allegory, mining the depths of ambiguity that could draw the viewers into a mirror of the complexities of their consciousness without paying heed to the academic tenets of political correctness. Simultaneously, these artists reinvented how to paint to make it reflect and merge with what they painted. The highly expressive brush stroke so long considered the hallmark of "serious" painting, from Willem de Kooning to Joan Mitchell to Georg Baselitz to Julian Schnabel, was suppressed or rejected in favor of more disciplined procedures, sometimes wildly decorative and obsessively crafted. The artists distanced themselves from their making in order better to serve their subjects, and their subjects often called a new visual originality into play—nowhere more so than in the work of four of the artists represented in *Fabulism*. The fifth artist, Carroll Dunham, had already begun his imaginary journey a decade or so earlier.

Some ten years or more the senior of the other four, Carroll Dunham literally and figuratively drew his way out of the Minimalist and Process Art of the 1960s and 1970s. Arriving in New York in 1972, he became the studio assistant of Dorothea Rockburne and absorbed the lessons of such artists as Mel Bochner and Barry Le Va. Dunham was strongly attracted to the painting of Brice Marden, Robert Ryman, and Robert Mangold. Slowly he twisted and turned this highly reductive painting, dependent upon the planar architecture of the canvas support, into an unlikely union with Surrealist automatism and dream imagery. Via the psychedelia of his 1960s youth, Dunham developed an interest in the most discredited side of Surrealism, the squirmy illusionism practiced by such as Matta and Yves Tanguy. In the early 1980s, his previously abstract linear doodles began to mime, grow out of, and transform the patterning of the wood veneer he now chose to work on. A kind of psychosexual delirium dependent upon the striations and knots of the wood plane erupted in intestinal, phallic, and vaginal allusions inflamed by a Looney Tunes palette. Like painter peers such as Terry Winters, Bill Jensen, and Philip Taaffe, Dunham was pushing abstraction toward figuration, but with an intensity and comic hilarity both unique and prescient. The queasy alliance his line formed between subjective, organic invention and objective interaction with the rectangularity of his painting plane has activated his work to the present day.

In 1988, Dunham returned to painting on linen, urging a pneumatic libidinal organism to funnel into the plane from the bottom physical edge of the support and surrounding it with vagrant galaxies of graffiti, including various written dates of its making and his signature. From a single color, this shape began to expand like a giant fungus on the linen host and became a raucous Technicolor *Mound* (1991–92). In subsequent works, this form began to mutate more and more toward the figurative, until these quasi-characters turned into a vagina dentata-mouthed demon. By 1997, mobs of glyphic, penis-nosed warriors and multi-breasted amazons battled for territory on the plane and the planet they polluted. With scabrous humor, scruffy paint, and incisive line, Dunham mocked and mimed our culture's mindless pillaging of the planet. Guston's startling turn, in the late 1960s, from Abstract Expressionism to schematic, comics-inspired figuration was crucial in setting the stage for not only Dunham's figuration but that of all the artists represented here, as well as countless others. However, in their flatness and hieratic rectangularity, Dunham's figures call more directly to Mayan wall painting, as well as to comics. No matter how obstreperous his characters become, they always remain creatures of and may even be entrapped by the rectangle they seek to conquer. Victim/victimizer, victor/vanquished.

Since 1997, a single figure, possibly a self-portrait, most often top-hatted, suited and starch-shirted, occasionally armed, penis-nosed when not headless, sometimes called *Killer,* has laid claim to Dunham's plane. In the last several years, this single figure has required Dunham's exclusive attention and represents him in this exhibition. A derelict painterliness, raw and impoverished of color, roils the *Mesokingdom* paintings (2001–02)—a painterliness, as in all of Dunham's work, in devotion to the painting's subject. Seen only upwards from shoulders pinioned, from painting to painting, to one or another outer edge of the plane, the figure bleeds in and out of the landscape, his top hat similar to and as disheveled as the shanties that dot the landscape. The trees echo the distressed eroticism of his testicular nostrils. He wears his landscape, or he is worn by the landscape. The prefix "meso" means intermediate; this is the kingdom of the intermediate, a kind of funky purgatory, a purgatory embroiled by a tour-de-farce variety of markmaking.

In the more recent (2003) *Personal Distance* works, the figure has cleaned up his act (or had it cleaned up) but has hardly improved his condition. Now flatly painted and graphically bordered in black, a still more fragmentary shoulders and/or head have been subjected to cold geometricization folded and ironed into and out of the plane of their making. Can the subject be as heroic as the scale of these paintings or is he enslaved by the heroics of his making? With hilarious pathos these works call back to the geometries of the 1960s and early 1970s, where Dunham began—and we are still left to ponder the meaning of in-between.

Like Dunham, Ellen Gallagher's art is very much drawing driven; and, like Dunham, she has subsumed elements of late modernism into her painting narrative, most specifically the grid that ruled much of 1960s art. Like so many of those of the 1960s, her grids mirror the rectangle of the painting plane; but unlike the abstract, self-reflexive geometries so previously prevalent, Gallagher's grids serve more allegorical functions—as containers, cells, or stages for clichés of old-time negritude. Quite magically and very quietly she has turned issues of race into a painting medium.

Agnes Martin, the most subjective of the 1960s geometers, became an early influence on Gallagher. Hardly out of Boston's School of the Museum of Fine Arts, in 1992 she replaced Martin's lyrically hand-executed grids bathed in transparent washes with myriads of sheets of mechanically lined penmanship papers pasted onto the surface of the canvas. Onto these sheets she drew countless big lips and/or bulging eyes that were hallmarks of the comic black impersonators performing in the Old South's minstrel shows. The resultant shimmering sea of monogrammatic clichés hovers somewhere between the handwritten and the printed, the visual and the verbal, markmaking and writing. The endless repetition of small increments draws the viewer into a slowly shifting meditative riff. The lips can be read as vagina as readily as mouth, maybe even as hot dog in a bun. Something erotic ripples across the plane. The repetitiveness both of the drawn elements and the lined paper might imply we are dealing with craft, craft impersonating painting, or vice versa. A gentle undermining seems to take place, an undermining of black clichés, an undermining of conventional notions of painting. Some times blacks took part in minstrel shows and impersonated whites impersonating blacks. Nothing is black and white, black or white.

In Gallagher's more recent work sampled here, the fragments of cliché physiognomy that become characters in and activate her paintings perform their ambiguities in spaces vast in scale and size. In *Purgatorium* (2000), an almost infinite repetition of lips is bordered on two sides by a sealike emptiness, here and there punctuated by amphibious, phallic spouts erupting and ejaculating out of the lined paper. Whether the lips are damned to an eternity of cliché or await a fuller, more individuated identity remains moot. We are enveloped by an epic that is lyrical, intimate, and full of questions.

Earlier in her life, Gallagher spent a summer at sea on a marine biology project; and the sea has played an important part in her life. Rolling umbel fragments of white-whalelike forms constructed out of cut-up penmanship paper float across the lined paper whiteness in *Blubber* and are accompanied by a tumbling school of flip wigs and eyes. Here, we might have arrived in the environs of *Moby Dick,* that astounding verbal epic admired by Gallagher, whose paintings, like Melville's writing, is made up of countless minuscule details slowly gathering into a monumental wave of ambiguous meaning. And all those bobbing, bewigged heads might call to the souls lost at sea during the days of slave trading.

Black, of course, takes on extra-aesthetic meaning when employed by an artist of color. And, partially, in response to critics who have faulted her for not making her content less ambiguous, less fluid, Gallagher has undertaken a number of monumental black paintings. The title *bling bling* (2001) refers to the clattering of excessive amounts of gold and diamond chains and rings associated with many a rap musician. The actual image is of another galaxy of stars, the Milky Way. The painting is obsessively constructed out of layers of penmanship paper, hand-cut pieces of rubber, and black enamel paint, and its reflective blackness makes it almost impossible to see other than as an enveloping wave of amorphous, black evanescence. Only the closest inspection reveals traces of the underlying grid and the repeated scattering of rubber eyeballs and tongues. We are left to ponder what is the identity that can be seen beyond the glittering of bling bling and whether our or anyone else's identity can be identified by its color. As viewers of art, we are given the opportunity to explore and understand our identity as we view ourselves in the ritualized reflections of the artist's consciousness.

Matthew Ritchie also charts epic tales. He has set out to do nothing less than remap the creation and evolution of the universe. With exuberance, humor, and high intelligence, he makes not only figurative but literal painting as the ground for thought. His is a multimedia enterprise, perhaps more installation than painting, that draws on science, religion, alchemy, myth, popular culture, the works.

After graduating from London's Camberwell School of Art in 1986, Ritchie embarked on his slacker years. In 1988, he moved to New York, took a job as a building superintendent, and pondered his options. Joseph Beuys' construction of a personal mythology and interest in art as a didactic tool had impressed him in school, as had the painting of Frank Stella and the enigmatic, alchemical metaphors created by Sigmar Polke. He observed what he thought to be the liberating effects of the breakdown of what he refers to as "the master narrative" (the all-white, mostly male modernist catechism) on artists like Julian Schnabel—anything was possible, any artist or style could be appropriated. In the midst of this heady, contextless anarchy, Ritchie felt the need to build a world, to recontextualize art. In short, he needed a new narrative. The art created by two of his peers spurred Ritchie on—the brilliant, acerbic silhouette cutouts that recontextualize tales of Southern whites' marginalization of blacks created by Kara Walker, and Matthew Barney's filmed and sculpted combinations of myth, magic, athletics, 1960s and 1970s body art, and more. Both Walker and Barney reinvented the elaborate historical narratives so prevalent in pre-modernist painting. And so Ritchie began to plot his narrative.

Voraciously curious, Ritchie spent countless hours reading books on science and philosophy that he found discarded in the environs of New York University. He began to see painting as a continuous flux, one that is not a creation of space but rather a concentration of information slowed down; and this flux mimes the continuous flux and upheavals of the universe. He imagined one continuous painting starting with the Big Bang and continuing ever forward into the present. By 1994, the materialization of this process began to crystallize.

With his first exhibition in 1995, Ritchie began to reinvent the grand history painting of pre-modernism. The number seven looms large in this world. Forty-nine elements divided into seven groups of seven. And each element can mutate into seven different ones, depending upon its interaction with the other elements. The forty-nine elements are characters with precisely defined functions. The plot can vary, characters can be added; all get absorbed into the continuous flux. Seven colors are employed, each corresponding to one of the seven areas of the brain. For instance, green represents the frontal lobe, the character Mulciber the builder, the sign Mu; black is the occipital lobe, Tamaii, Ta. Seven representational modes are employed in this endeavor: drawing, photography, sculpture, wall painting, painting on canvas, published texts, and digital media.

Quite unbelievably, the information overload called into play by Ritchie is embodied in vibrant clarity and joyousness. The basis of his ongoing project is usually one or more paintings on canvas depicting countless varieties of intertwining swirling and twisting waves of his seven unmodulated colors and trailing hundreds of shards and fragments of tumult—a kind of archeology of the tracks of creation and destruction. Emerging from these vectors of energy, almost like fleeting hallucinations, are delicately drawn comic personifications of various of the forty-nine elements, scientific equations, and occasional bits of writing. Extending around the wall from the painting and onto the floor are more diagrammatically constructed whorls of colored waves, either created with paint or a Formica-like substance (Sintra) that draw the viewer into the vortex of Ritchie's world. The written text (often a small published pamphlet) accompanying this visual excess is wonderfully written in old-time whodunit noir, full of intrigue and gambling, and likely to combine a Golem and an astronaut and countless other characters with multiple identities, such as Bubba, who is Beelzebub, the principal of growth and Planck's constant. And photographs of scientific phenomena, or Miami's Eden Roc Hotel, and tables of Ritchie's elements, and diagrams, and reproductions of limpid watercolors—all adding still more layers to Ritchie's narrative. So, too, does his interactive website, where the player can test his or her wits with one or more element/character. Einstein meets Japanese *anime* meets the Old Testament meets pulp fiction meets William of Ockham meets Frank Stella, and on and on and on.

The viewer is free to interact with as much or as little of this concentration of information as he or she chooses. At the time of this writing, Ritchie is still composing his installation for Joslyn; so, happily, you are on your own. The more we study, the richer the world becomes. In the free-floating multiplicity of the world without a dominant narrative in which we find ourselves, we tend to not know the iconography of medieval European and Italian Renaissance painting much better than we know the continuously morphing gods of Hindu art. With inquiry and study, visual beauty is likely to accumulate more profound density, whether facing the monkey god Hanuman leading his simian warriors on a relief at Angkor Wat, or Matthew Ritchie's churning universe. His characters' polymorphously shifting identity is not dissimilar to the multiple identities made possible by the internet. His startling conjunctions of different systems of information are not dissimilar to the seemingly discontinuous overload of information we are confronted with when flipping channels on the television remote or paging through the newspaper. Ritchie embraces this incredibly complicated world and urges us into his fluid narrative.

Like Ritchie's macrocosmic creation as metaphor for the artist's microcosmic creation, Neo Rauch's paintings might be read as metaphors for making. However, "might" is the operative word here. More inscrutable and more opaquely painted, Rauch's world is frozen in incompletion and filled with troubling disruptions and pauses. Hypnotically his figures move; enigmatically they construct. Born into the slow death throes of East Germany's socialism in 1960, Rauch has, amongst much else, turned the promise of socialist realism upside down. However, his figures are not localized but enact more universal, allegorical disjunctions. Rauch is drawn to such conjurers of disturbed entrancement as Max Beckmann, Balthus, Francis Bacon, and Georg Baselitz.

Rauch's early work includes a number of large (some ten feet in diameter), irregular tondos sparsely composed in quadrants of distressed, faded color, fragmented space inhabited by one or two puppetlike gnomes performing odd acts of devotion and/or something torturous, and one or more words in block letters that may or may not be germane to the activity represented. The paint has physically troubled the paper surface with wrinkles, lumps, and creases. In 1995, this dark world moved into more ample, detailed landscape spaces often disrupted by and disrupting fragmentary, obsolete factory buildings and machinery, and just as often disrupting and disrupted by somnambulistic, mostly male laborers wielding improbable tools (sabers, something like hockey sticks, unwieldy lengths of poles, etc.) and performing improbable tasks forever doomed to incompletion. Rauch's manner of painting is the most conventionally figurative of *Fabulism*'s participants: clear, spare execution with short, assured strokes, no more paint than necessary to the representation of the subject, even light, complexity of composition as assured and clear as the handling of paint. He is a brilliant painter. Most of the figures he paints are sturdy, Nordic males who would easily be capable of performing social-realistic tasks of stalwart work and goodness. One of the males frequently recurring in Rauch's paintings may or may not be a self-portrait. All of the males perform dysfunctionally. The quandary of their movements and surroundings suggest something far more than the breakdown of socialism that took place during Rauch's growing up.

As precise as Rauch's conundrums appear, they are not predetermined. He starts with tiny preliminary sketches, then outlines the basics of his initial compositional thoughts on the canvas and begins to dream his way into the painting, urging the painting to dream on into an organic totality, not entirely knowing until after that totality has been achieved what he has painted. Although slower, more painstaking, and less revelatory of the process of making than Dunham often is, Rauch, like Dunham, submits to the climate of his intuition. He paints from the inside out. Inside becomes outside and vice versa. The low-lying landscape seen in many of Rauch's paintings is drawn from the familiar surroundings of his native Leipzig into the unfamiliar, as is the disheveled architecture. The faded pastels so often pervading his palette are based on colors remembered from childhood.

The title, *Neid,* of a painting created in 1999 hovers in the empty fireplace of the interior depicted on the right-hand side. The word is a protagonist as hard to explain as the giant fungi beneath it and those growing from the large timbers on either side of the fireplace, and as hard to explain as the dark sod or moss hanging from the ceiling. A tense, electric light fills the room and the mirror over the fireplace with pallid green. The two male occupants seem trapped in the overbearing rectilinearity of their interior, taking no note of the erosion of that interior inflicted by fungi and moss. And on the left side of the canvas invades an inexplicable cascade of planes, maybe shelflike, maybe referring to an obsolete industrial process, maybe to 1960s Minimalist monochromatic painting or an exploding Donald Judd sculpture. As mutely frozen as the painting seems, the eye is drawn in and around over and over again, constantly trying to construct a narrative, to make connections, to understand the meaning of a previously unseen detail, maybe getting jealous of the certainty of the word that means "jealousy" in German. But there are other words in other paintings hovering just as certainly and ultimately having their meaning questioned by their surroundings. In many ways the viewer re-enacts the subject's striving for coherence in a world that has none, seeking meaning, floating on the edge of comprehension, bemoaning the loss of modernist utopianism, performing acts that no longer can be productive but must be enacted nonetheless. Seeking comprehension, while knowing none can be found. Like Beckmann's spiky, toxic beauty, Rauch's viral stillness silently guides our quest.

Occasionally, landscape alone embodies Rauch's dreaming. As in most of his paintings, *Acker* (2002) provides no kinesthetic entrance for the viewer's body but only space for the eye to roam. The swath of mining-wounded land at the bottom of the canvas blocks the imaginary entrance of the viewer's body and leaves the eye to seek its own path. The painting becomes a stage performed upon by the artist's conscious/unconscious will and the viewer's eye's mind. One must struggle like the starved weeds straining to grow out of the disruption of the ground. Seldom has a landscape been so still and so fraught. In one of his most recent paintings, *Haus des Lehrers* (2003), more expansive in scale, space, palette, and troubling depth, we witness the corrosive commingling of landscape, architecture, and figures that more frequently enact Rauch's puzzles. Strange bacterial growths envelop scattered household furnishings and tree stumps, swallowing books of learning as two male figures look on in stunned silence. Has learning infected nature, we might wonder, or could the painting be an oracle from which we have not yet learned to ask the right question?

The vivid exuberance of Chris Ofili's paintings might at first convince us that he, unlike Rauch, is dealing with more certainty. However, the only thing that might be said unequivocally about his work is its joyous embrace of beauty. Like Ellen Gallagher, his subjects deal with clichés of blackness; and, like her meticulous collaging and cutting, Ofili's multiplicity of obsessively repetitive and precisely placed collage elements approaches craft—as does his excessive decorativeness. Ofili, however, is as brashly direct as Gallagher is cryptic. His choice of subject matter has turned to the gaudier side of how blacks are perceived by others and themselves. However, he undermines the very clichés he celebrates. The rhythmic thumping, exaggerated sexualization, lavish sparkling, and hyper artificiality that swirl so precisely through his paintings call to the hip hop musicians like Lil' Kim, Foxy Brown, and Wu-Tang Clan he adores and occasionally iconicizes, and to the pimp and gangster paradise of 1970s blaxploitation movies. But this same artist grew up a Catholic, was once an altar boy and seems to believe in the possibility of a hip hop heaven. The visionary William Blake resides in Ofili's pantheon, as do Philip Guston, Francis Picabia, Sigmar Polke, and Ofili's jazz-obsessed predecessor, Jean-Michel Basquiat. This artist who so gleefully turns his back on the pieties of political correctness is

Bible-knowledgeable and was inspired by Blake to create one of his first figurative paintings, *Satan* (1995). Irony and sincerity, religion and pornography, seduction and irritation, abstraction and figuration are collaged into his work.

In 1992, while still at the Royal College of Art in London, Ofili traveled to Africa—a trip that fertilized his beginnings not only with elephant dung but also with the repetitive patterns of dots he saw in the cave paintings in the Matopos hills of Zimbabwe and with many things that have no physical form. Africa is, of course, where humans first evolved, made marks that had no practical function, and developed language. Upon his return to London, inspired both by his African sojourn and by the brilliant American trickster David Hammons, who in 1978 had made a sculpture of a three-wheeled mound of elephant dung and in 1983 had set up a stall selling snowballs, Ofili set up a stall on the streets for the exhibit of elephant dung, placed an "Elephant Shit" ad in the art magazine *Frieze,* and made a sculpture out of a dung ball and his own hair. While this Dada Voodoo phase was short-lived, this conflation of new Afro and traditional tribal African creating would be absorbed in Ofili's subsequent work.

Like Dunham, Ofili's first mature paintings are abstract, amongst them *Painting with Shit on It* (1993). Pulsing with thousands of tiny, dimensional, oil-painted dots in whorls of concentric circles intertwining with transparent rectangles, studded with a resin-dripping dung ball, and propped on the floor on two more dung balls, the super-obsessive, ritualized beauty of this painting serves as the door into Ofili's world. By 1995, his paintings propped up on dung began to take a more figurative turn that turned into full frontal figuration with his now infamous *The Holy Virgin Mary* (1996) and the first of the *Captain Shit and the Legend of the Black Stars* paintings, amongst which is the painting created in 2000 shown here, *The Naked Spirit of Captain Shit and the Legend of the Black Stars.* Captain Shit is the swaggering super hero inspired by the 1970s blaxploitation films that have so heavily impacted hip hopdom; by various black and white comic book heroes, including Spiderman, Black Panther, Black Lightning; and by Andy Warhol's Elvis (who was, in turn inspired by swiveling black musicians). This imposing figure is surrounded by black stars and partially encircled by dung balls (four, each with a white star, and one with the monogram BS that forms the Captain's belt buckle) and, of course, is endowed with a mythic penis. The pale, creamy ground has been painted with phosphorescent paint; and when the lights go out, Captain Shit fades into the background and is all but obliterated by the black stars. The macho star is vaporized and recedes into an insubstantial illusion. The cliché is celebrated, questioned, then dissolved in light. First impressions are deceiving.

A group of Ofili's paintings begun in 1999 and continuing through 2002 celebrates a kind of monkey king and ends with a glowing chapel-like installation of twelve paintings of individual monkeys that are the participants in the Last Supper. Two paintings created early on in this group bring their joyous pomp into this exhibition. Ofili is entranced by light and sparkle (bling bling, again) and his paintings can be as opulent as a bejeweled Gothic reliquary; but his sparkling, jeweled excess, as we see here, is fabricated from the shine of the dots of oil paint, glitter, map pins, and resin. The models for these paintings are Rhesus Macaque monkeys known to be loud and active pranksters with highly developed dexterity. For the purpose of research, these monkeys were introduced into an island off Puerto Rico, now known as "Monkey Island," and there they enchanted Ofili. Does the prankster monkey's dexterity suggest a surrogate for the artist, or does the prankster play with another cliché of blackness?

There is no proper end here. All five of these artists are somewhere in mid career. Already they have added new chapters to art's most malleable medium, perhaps the medium capable of greatest depth. They are here not to give us answers but to make us wonder as they create wonders.

KLAUS KERTESS

August 2003

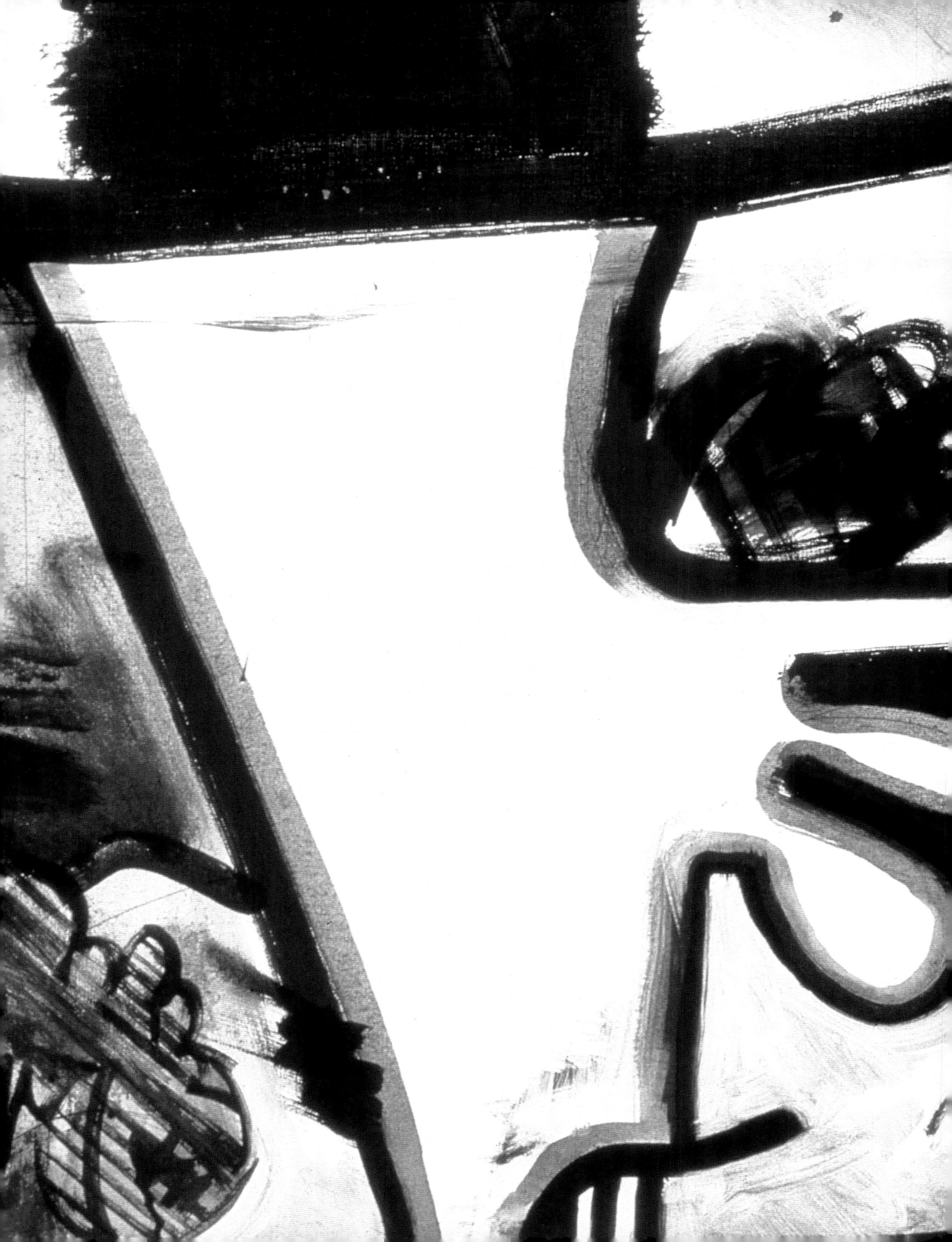

CARROLL DUNHAM

Mesokingdom One

2001, mixed media on linen, 80 x 64 inches (203.2 x 162.6 cm)

COLLECTION OF THE ARTIST

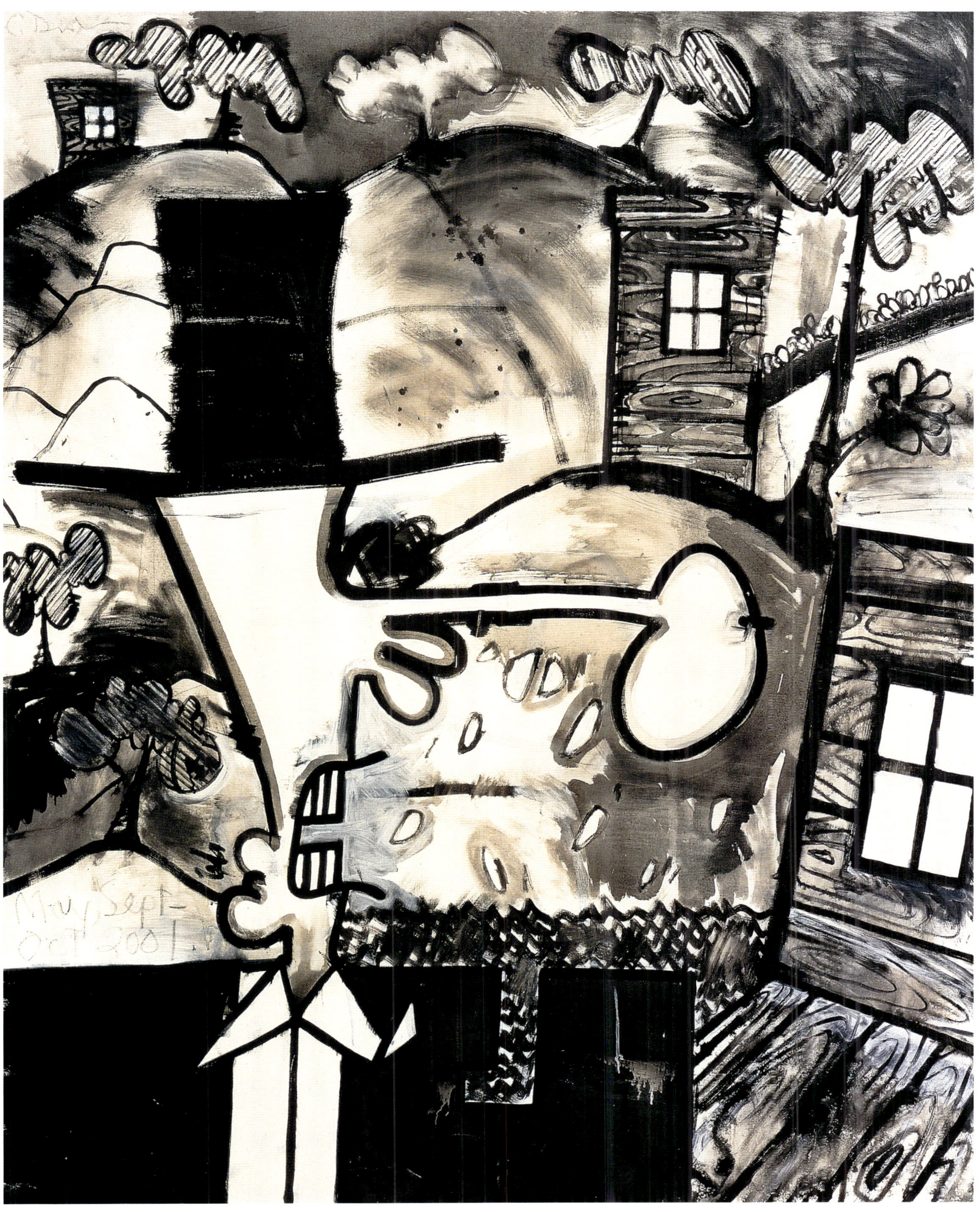
May, Sept-
Oct 2001

Shade

2000–02, mixed media on linen, 80 x 74 inches (203.2 x 188 cm)

COLLECTION OF THE ARTIST

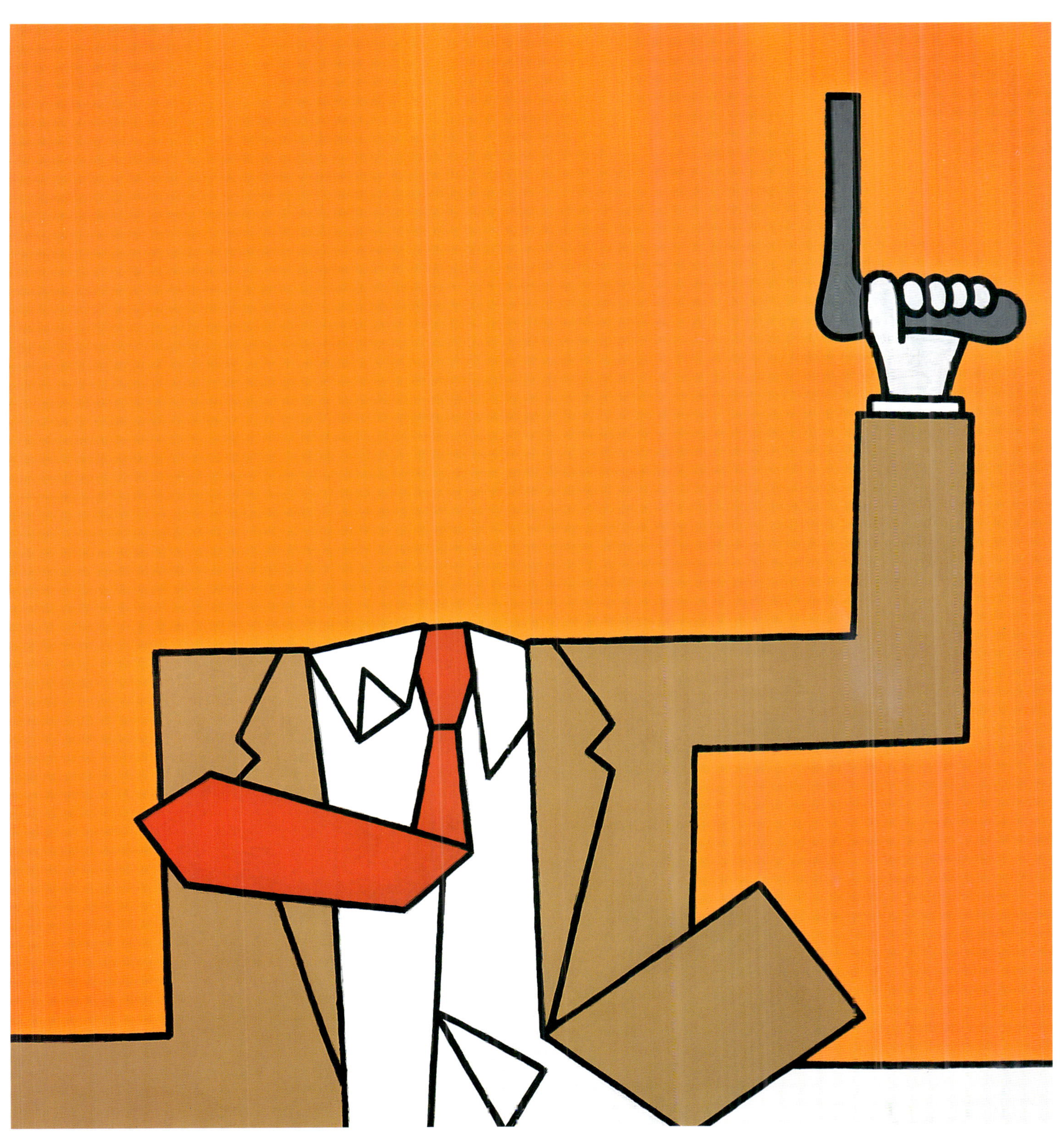

Mesokingdom Fourteen (Edge of Night)

2002, mixed media on linen, 96 x 93 inches (243.8 x 236.2 cm)

COLLECTION OF TERRI AND PHIL SCHRAGER, OMAHA

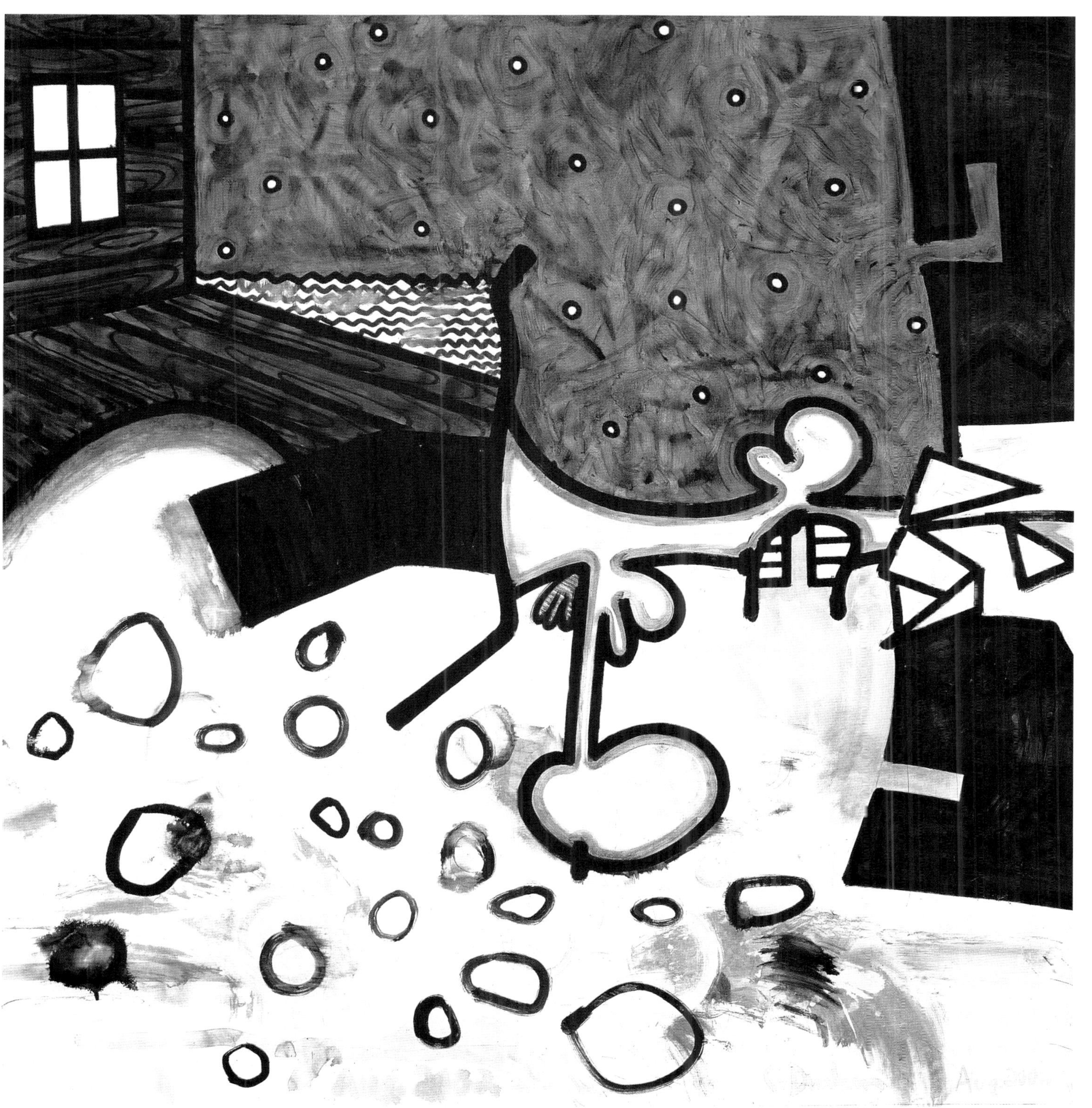

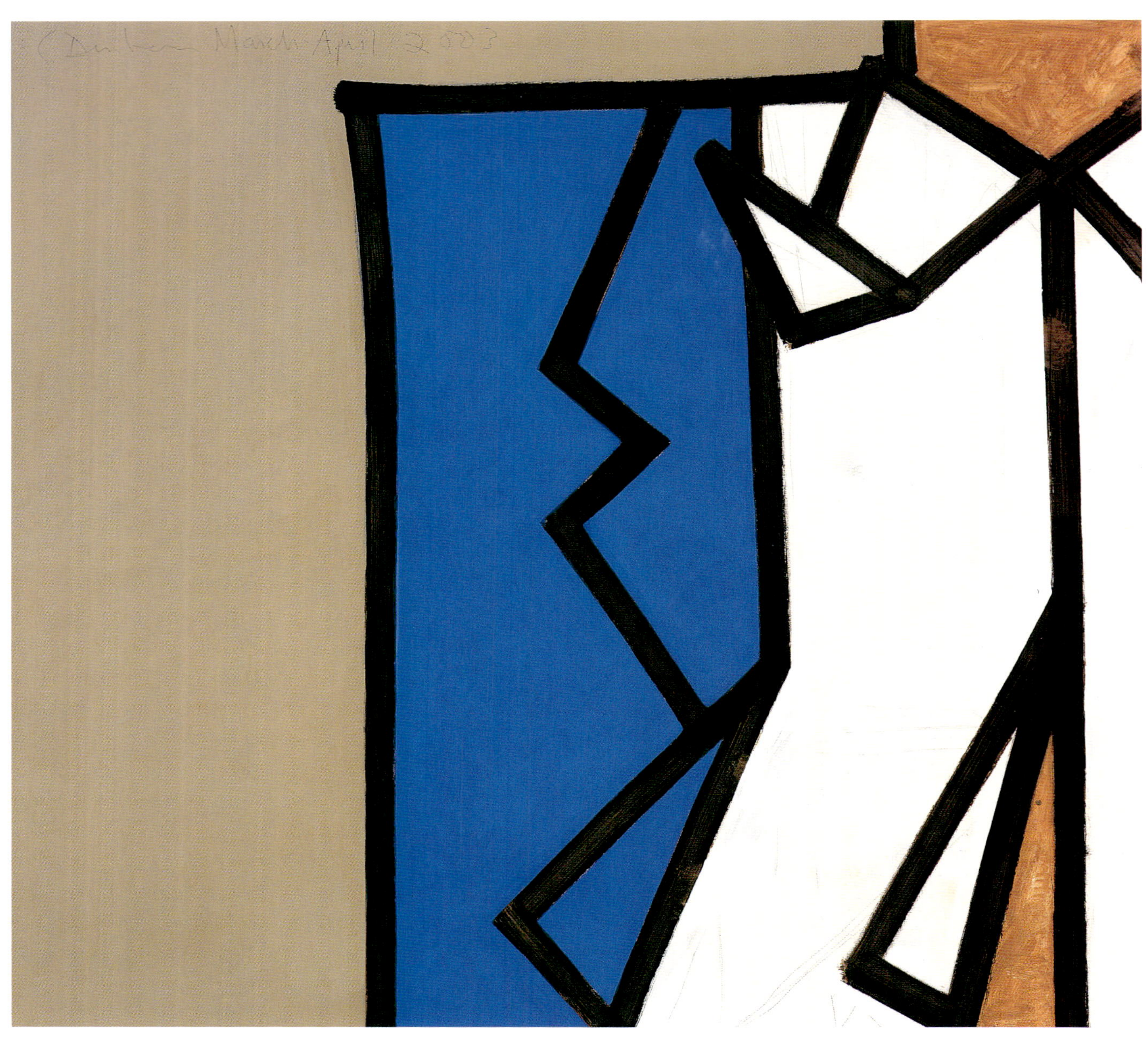

Personal Distance (One)

2003, mixed media on linen, 70 x 77 inches (177.8 x 195.6 cm)

COLLECTION OF LAUREN AND TIM SCHRAGER, ATLANTA

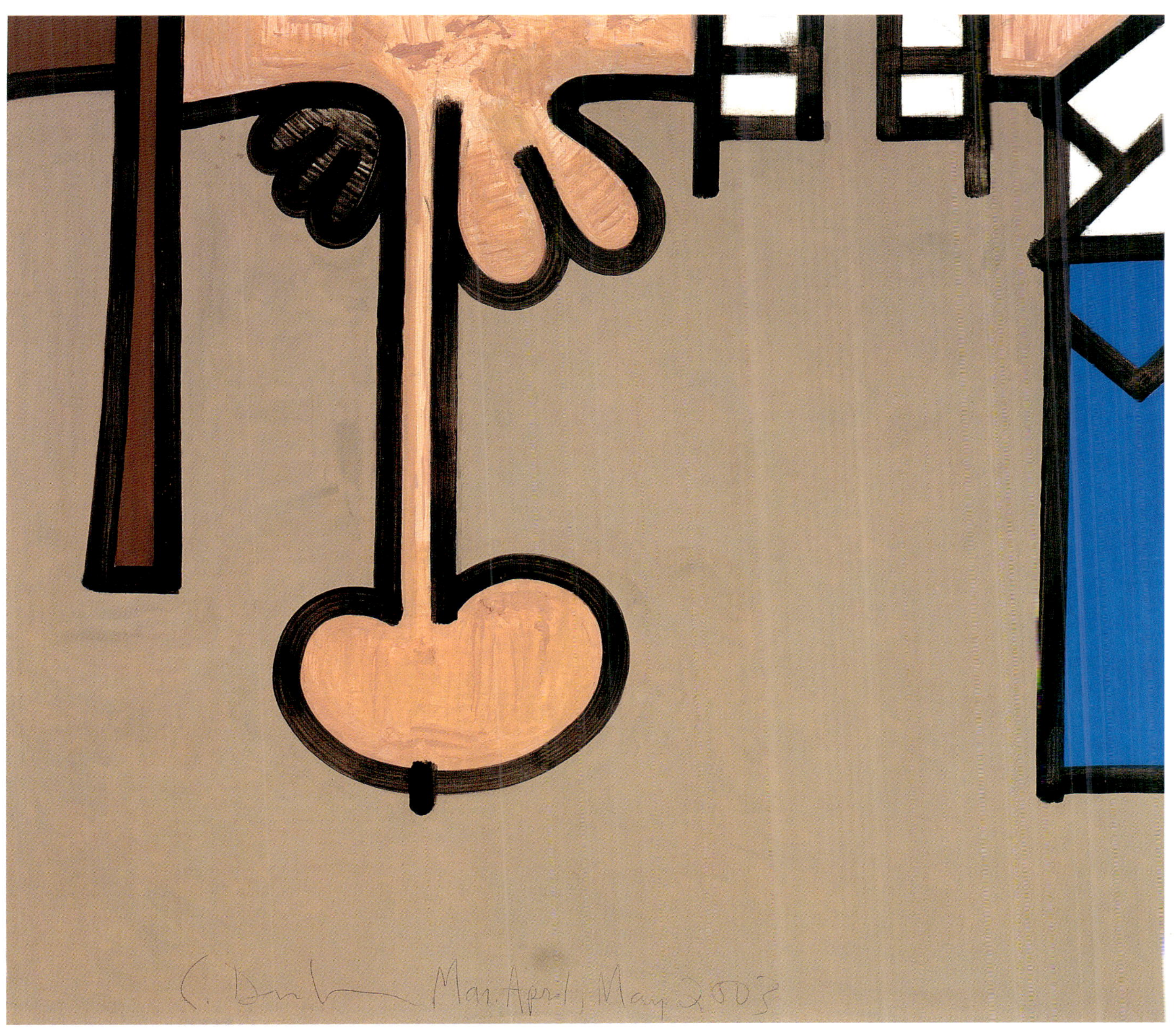

Personal Distance (Two)

2003, mixed media on linen, 72 x 81 inches (182.9 x 205.7 cm)

COLLECTION OF TERRI AND PHIL SCHRAGER, OMAHA

ELLEN GALLAGHER

Purgatorium

2000, ink, pencil, plasticine, and paper on linen, 120 x 96 inches (304.8 x 243.8 cm)

COLLECTION OF THE ARTIST

OVERLEAF: *Blubber*

2000, ink, pencil, and paper on linen, 120 x 192 inches (304.8 x 487.7 cm)

[not included in exhibition]

THE ART MUSEUM AT PRINCETON UNIVERSITY

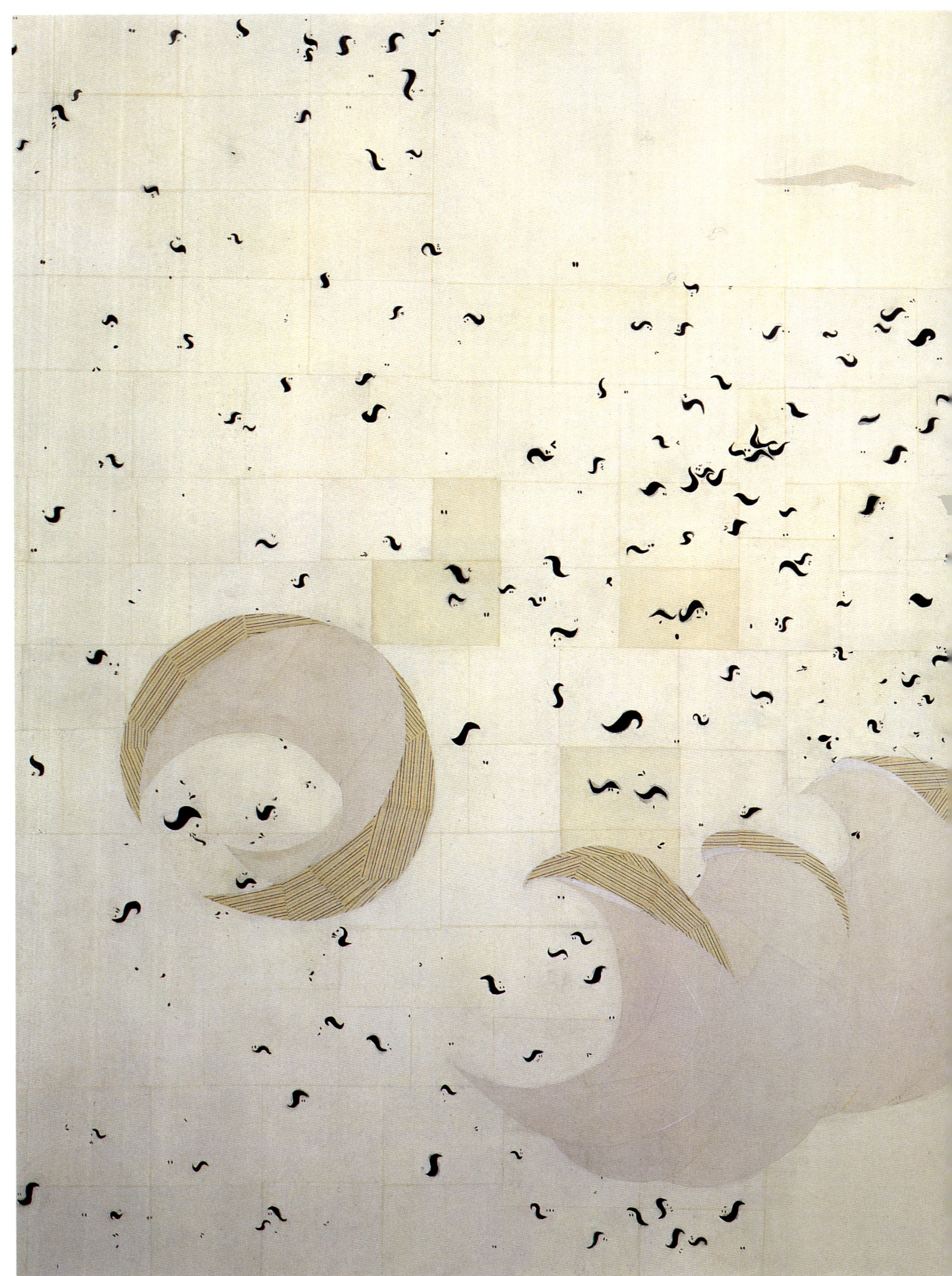

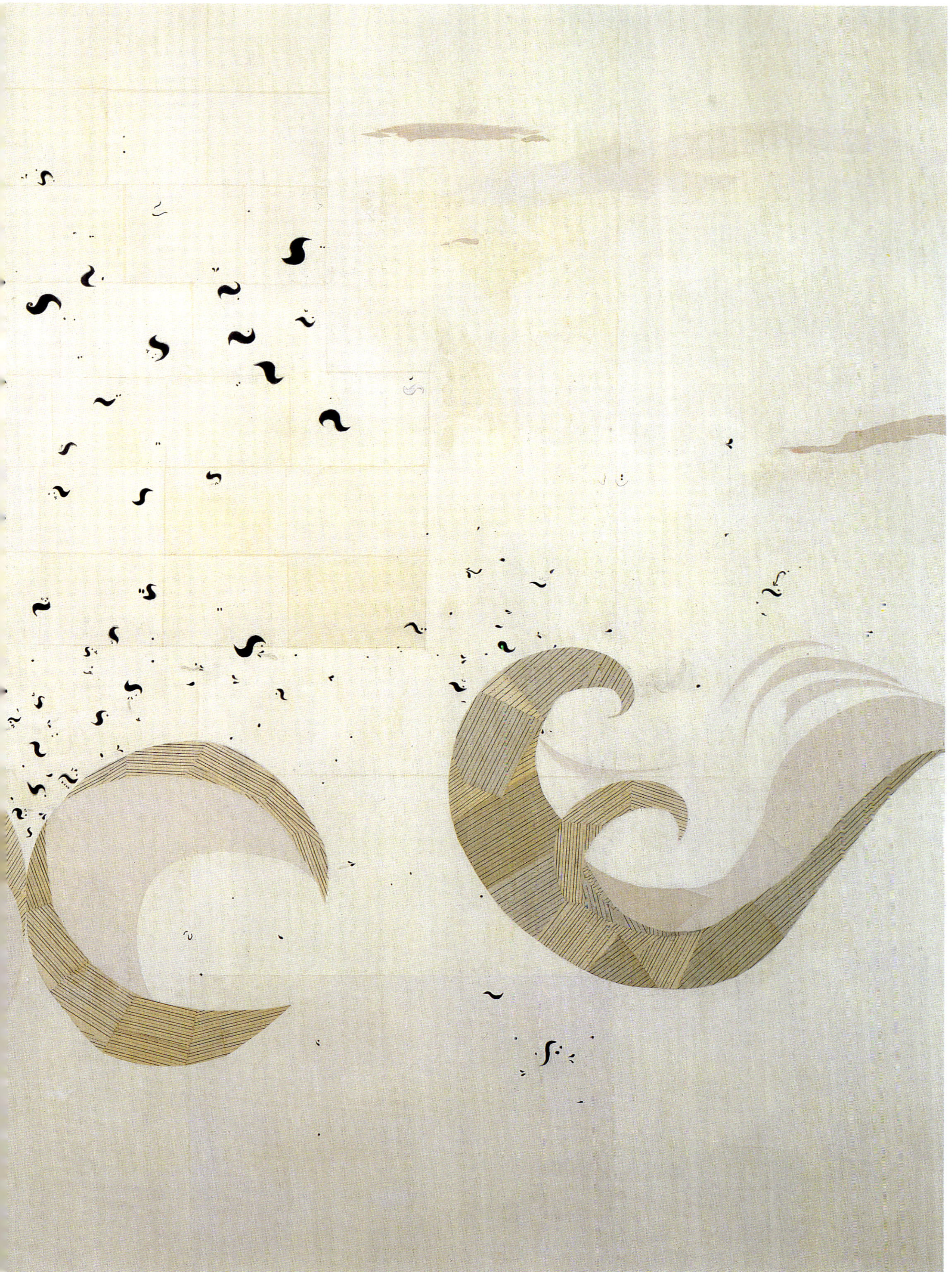

ly

2000, oil, ink, plasticine, and paper on linen, 72 x 84 inches (182.9 x 213.4 cm)

PURCHASED WITH FUNDS FROM THE COFFIN FINE ARTS TRUST;

NATHAN EMORY COFFIN COLLECTION OF THE DES MOINES ART CENTER, 2001.2

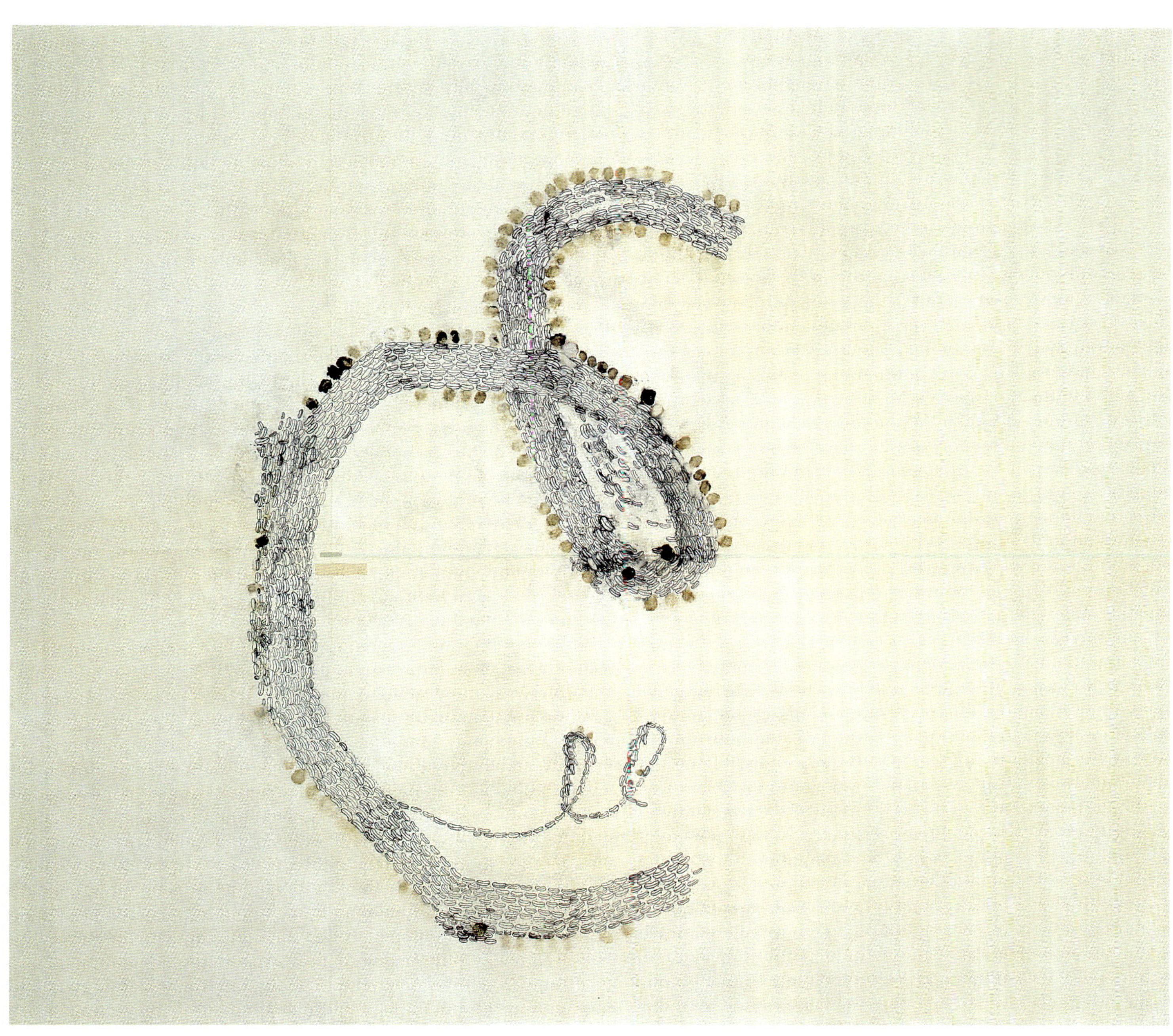

bling bling

2001, enamel, rubber, and paper on linen, 96 x 120 inches (243.8 x 304.8 cm)

THE BROAD ART FOUNDATION, SANTA MONICA

Psychoalphadiscobetabioaquadoloop

2001, paper, cut rubber, and enamel on canvas,
96 x 120 inches (243.8 x 304.8 cm)

COLLECTION OF THE ARTIST

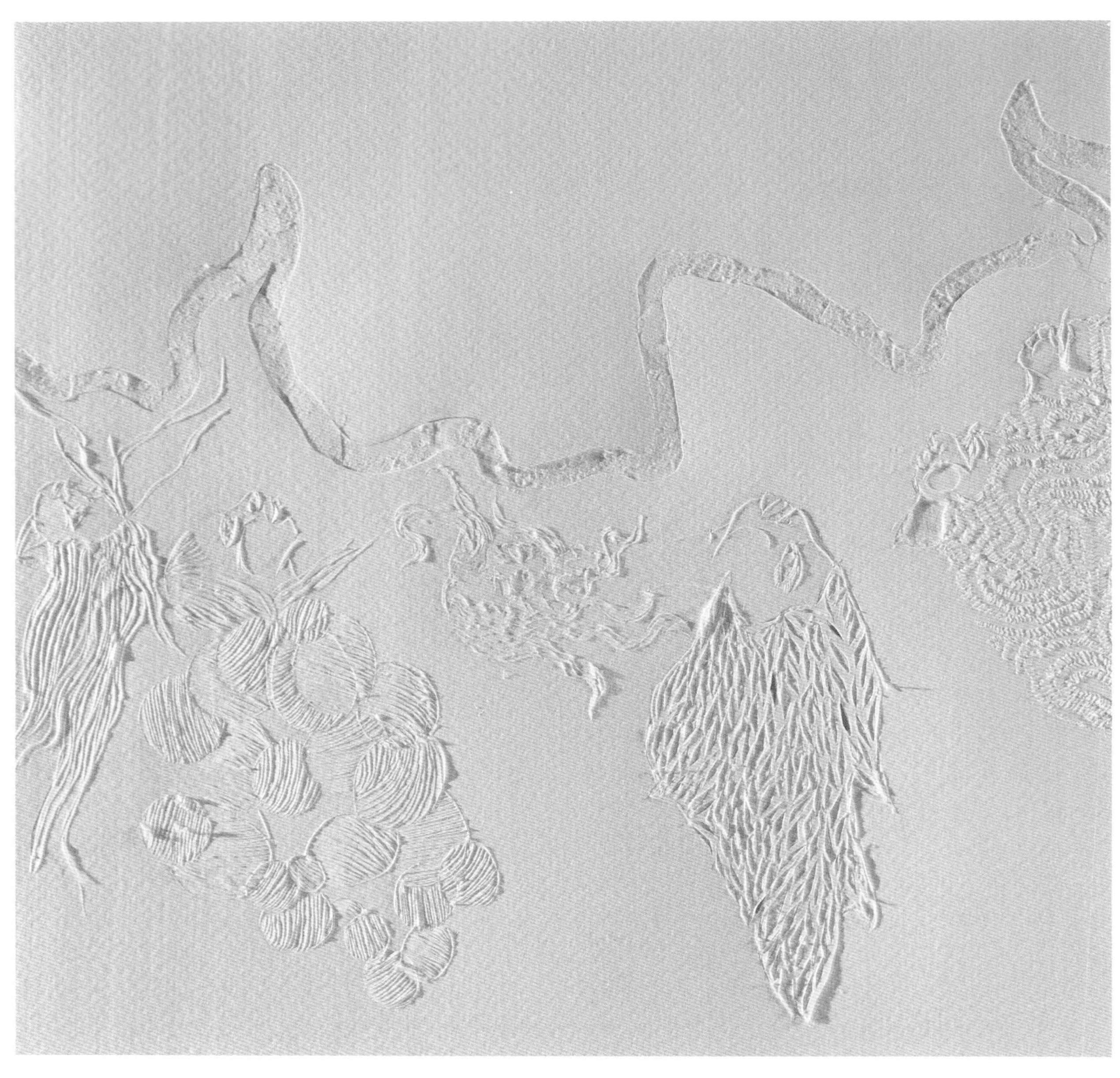

Watery Ecstatic (1 00 N, 7 00 E) [detail]
2003, cut paper, 60¼ x 74 inches (153 x 188 cm)

COLLECTION OF THE ARTIST
COURTESY GAGOSIAN GALLERY

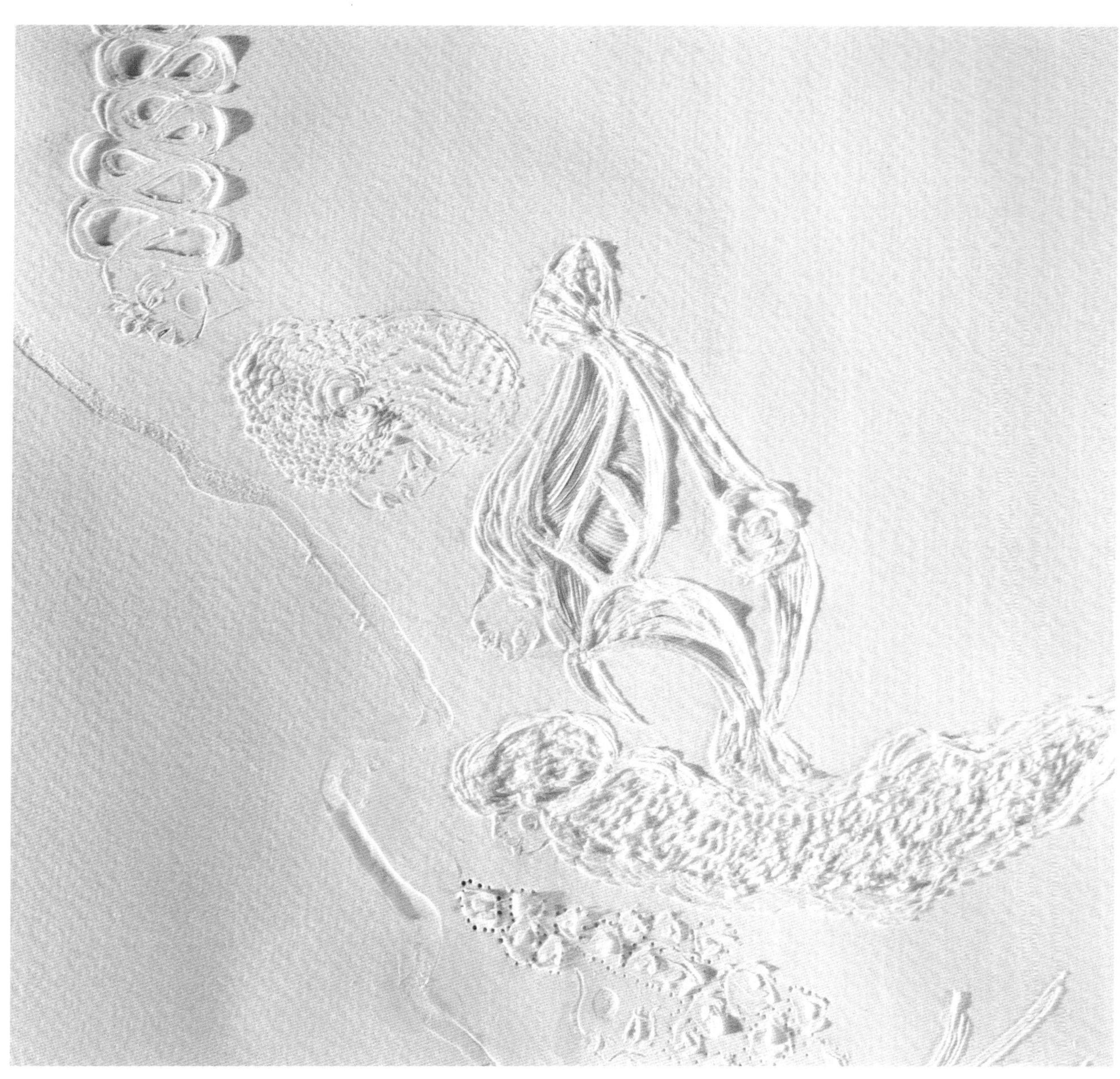

Watery Ecstatic (21 06 S, 53 36 E) [detail]
2003, cut paper, 60¼ x 74 inches (153 x 188 cm)

COLLECTION OF THE ARTIST
COURTESY GAGOSIAN GALLERY

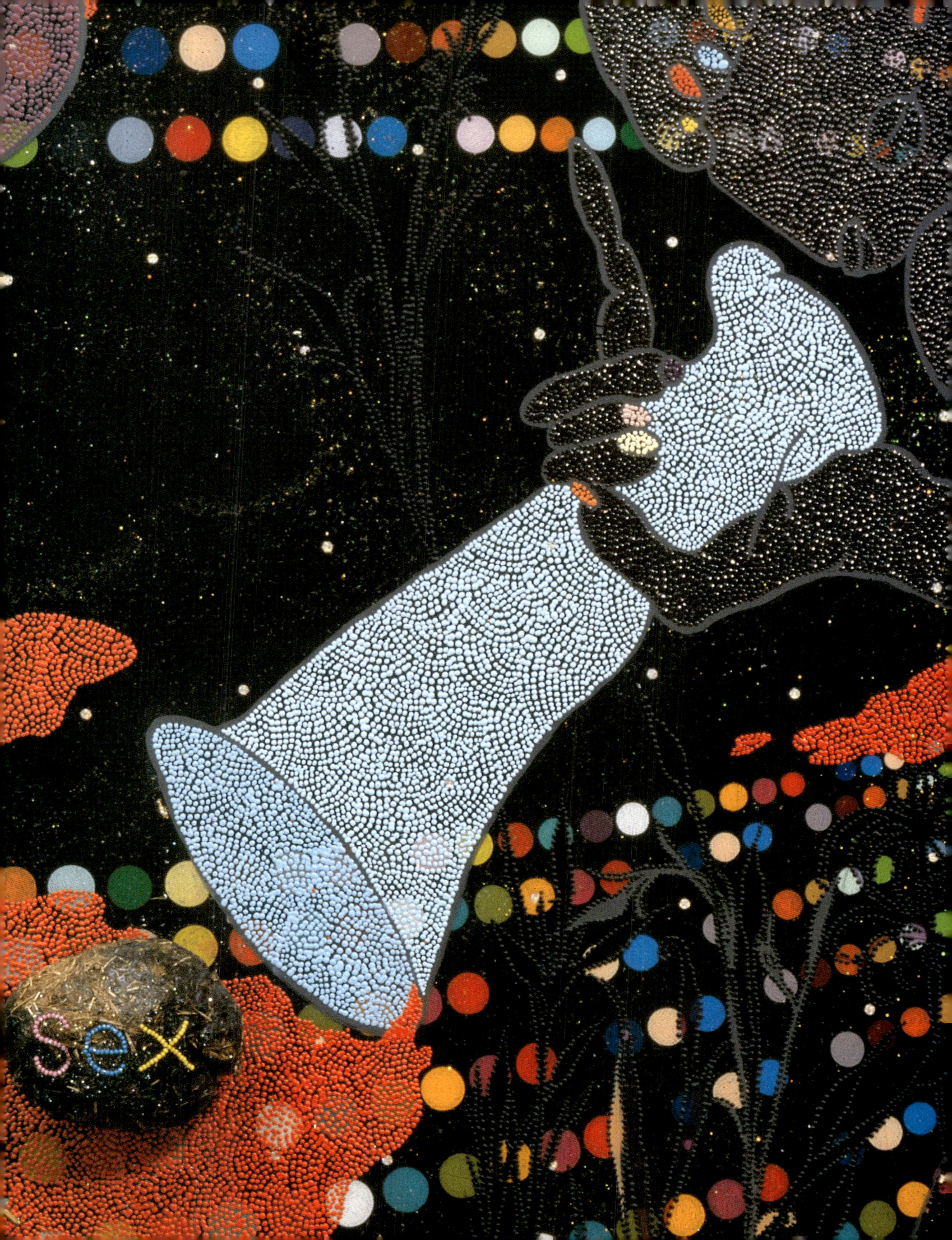

sex

CHRIS OFILI

Monkey Magic—Sex, Money and Drugs
1999, acrylic, collage, glitter, resin, pencil, map pins, and elephant dung on canvas, with two elephant dung supports, 96 x 72 inches (243.8 x 183 cm).

THE MUSEUM OF CONTEMPORARY ART, LOS ANGELES, PURCHASED WITH FUNDS PROVIDED BY THE BROAD ART FOUNDATION

OVERLEAF: *Dead Monkey—Sex, Money and Drugs*
2001, acrylic, oil, resin, map pins, and elephant dung on linen, with two elephant dung supports, 72 x 120 inches (183 x 304.8 cm)

COLLECTION OF TERRI AND PHIL SCHRAGER, OMAHA; PROMISED GIFT TO JOSLYN ART MUSEUM

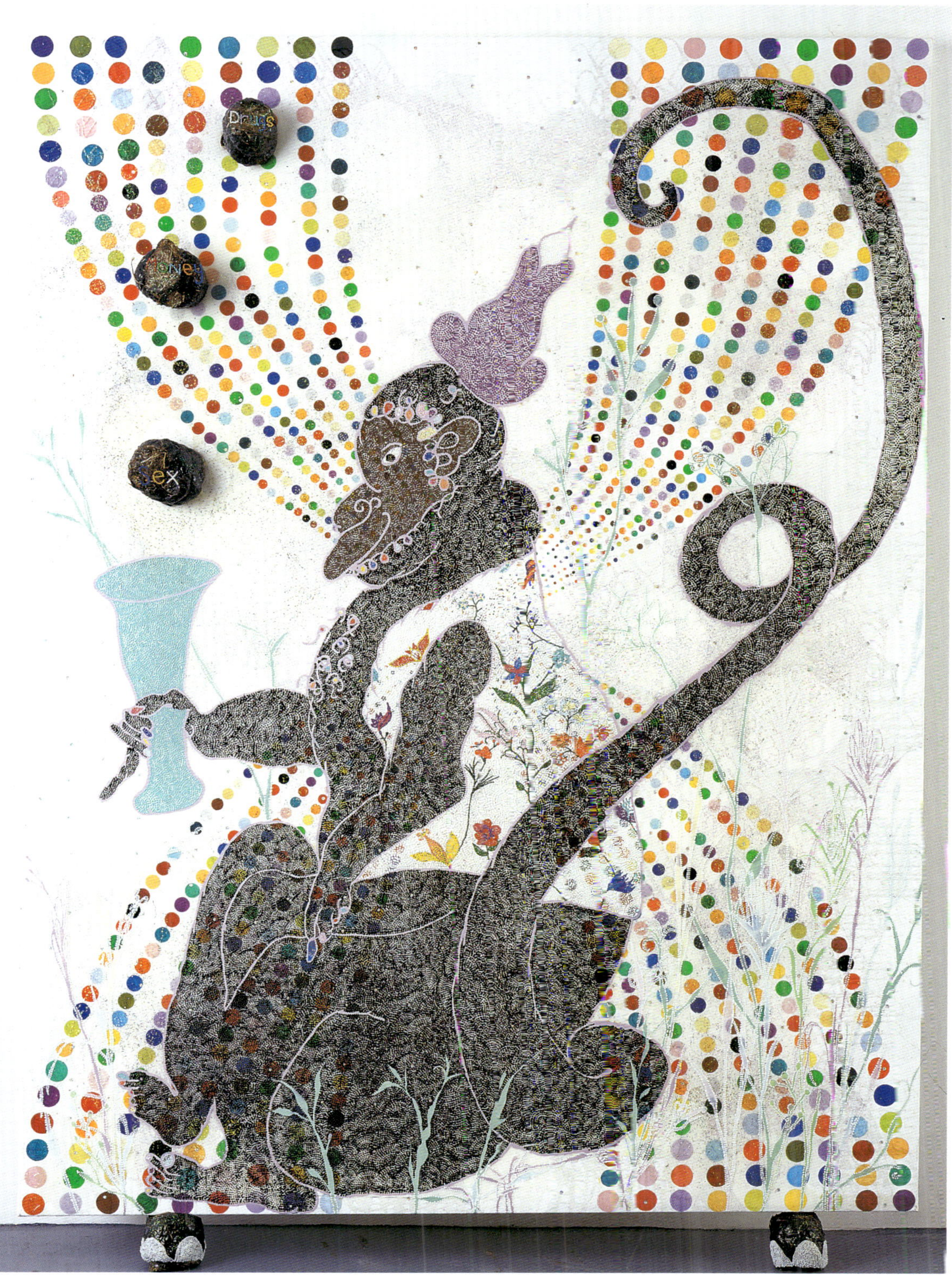
Drugs
Money
Sex

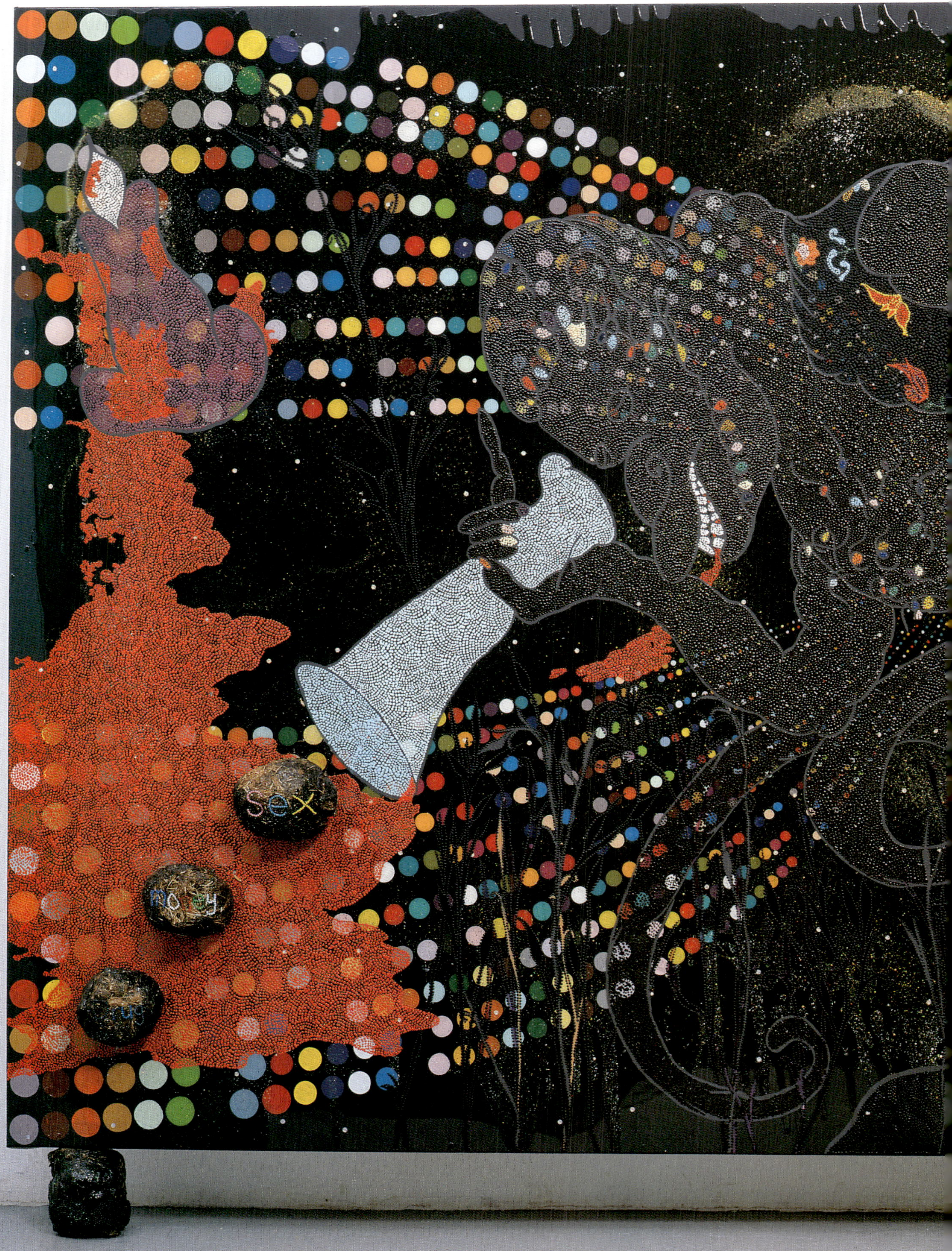
sex

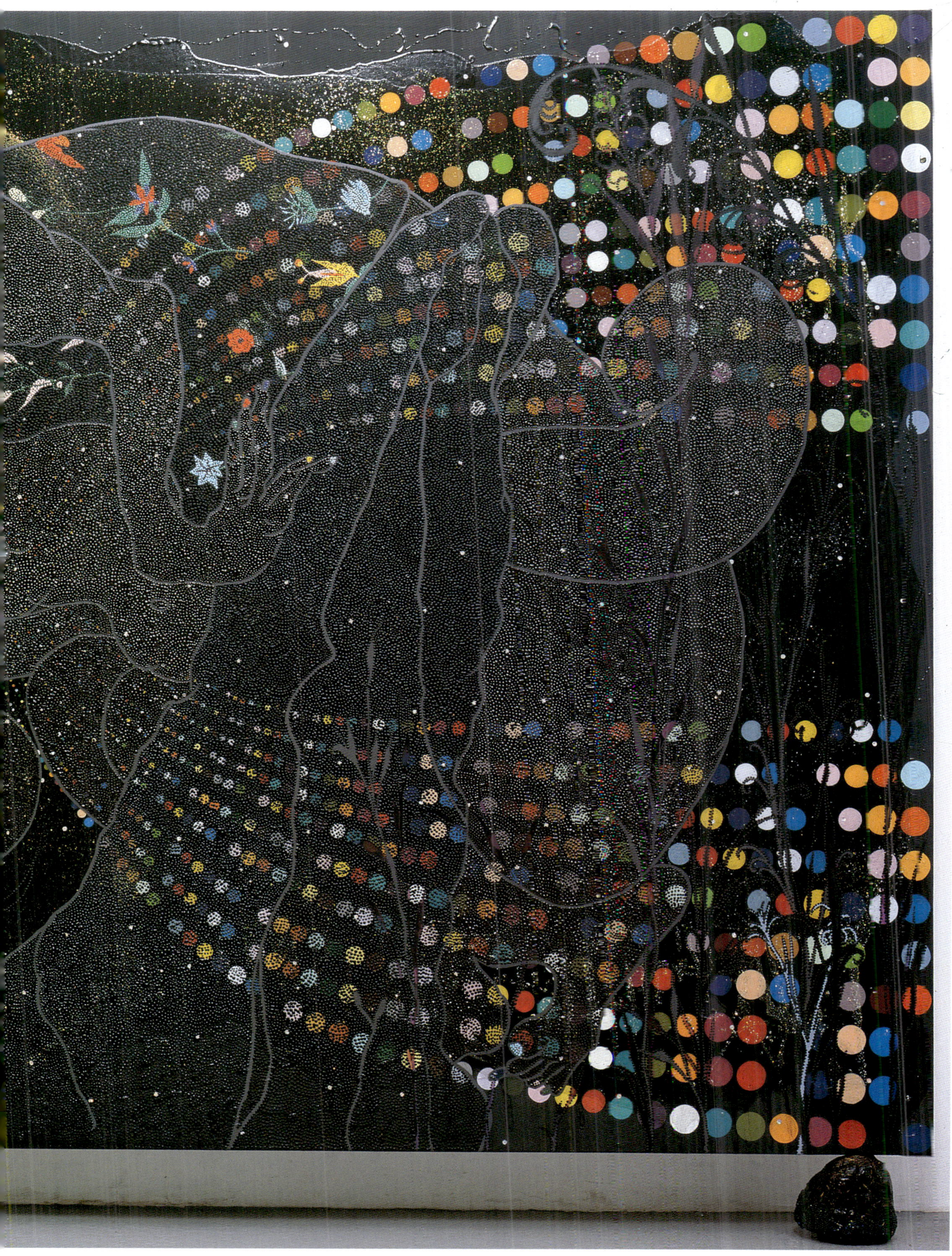

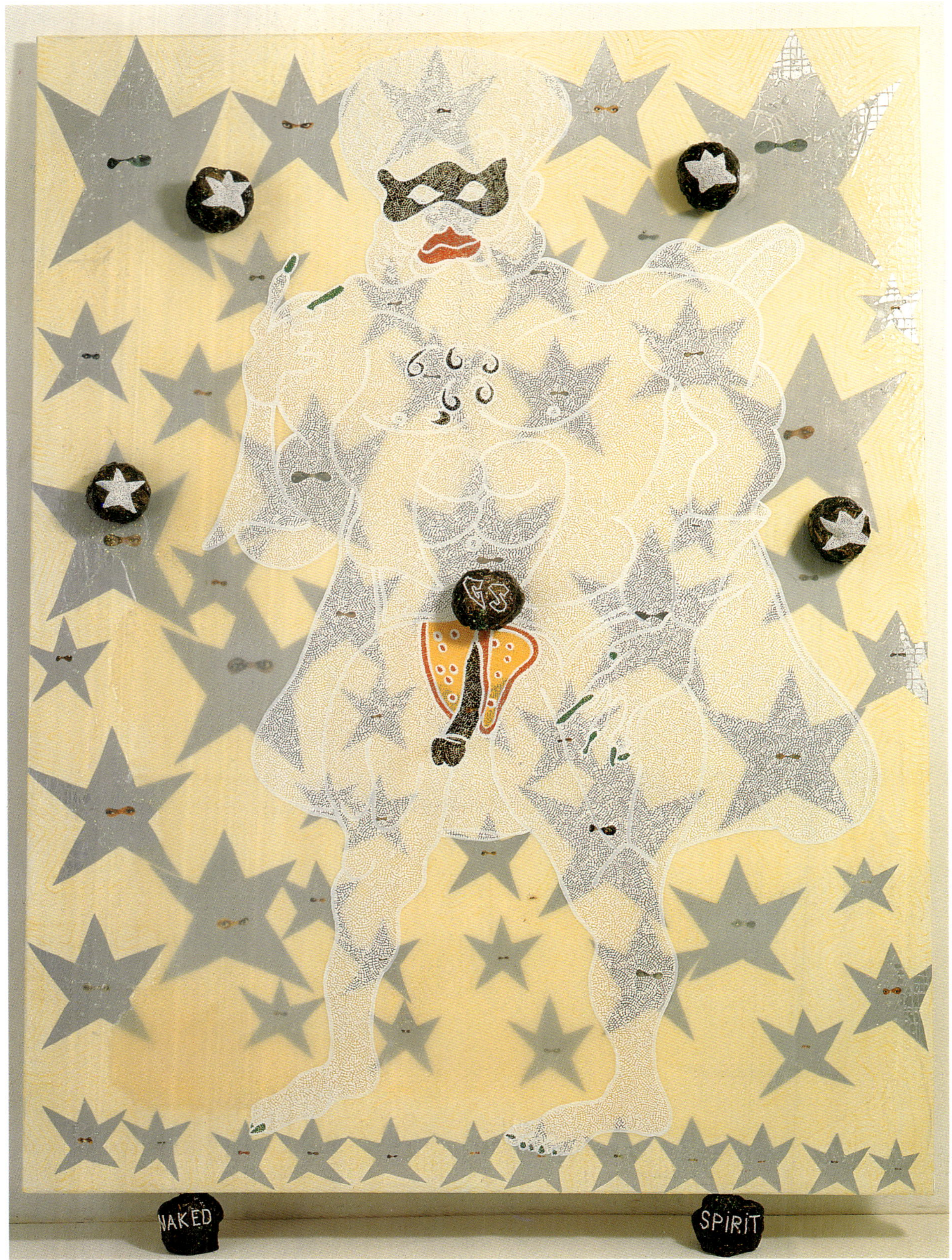

The Naked Spirit of Captain Shit and the Legend of the Black Stars

ABOVE: lights on; OPPOSITE: lights off

2000, acrylic, collage, glitter, resin, map pins, and elephant dung on canvas, with two elephant dung supports, 96 x 72 inches (243.8 x 183 cm)

COLLECTION OF IVELIN AND CRAIG ROBINS, MIAMI

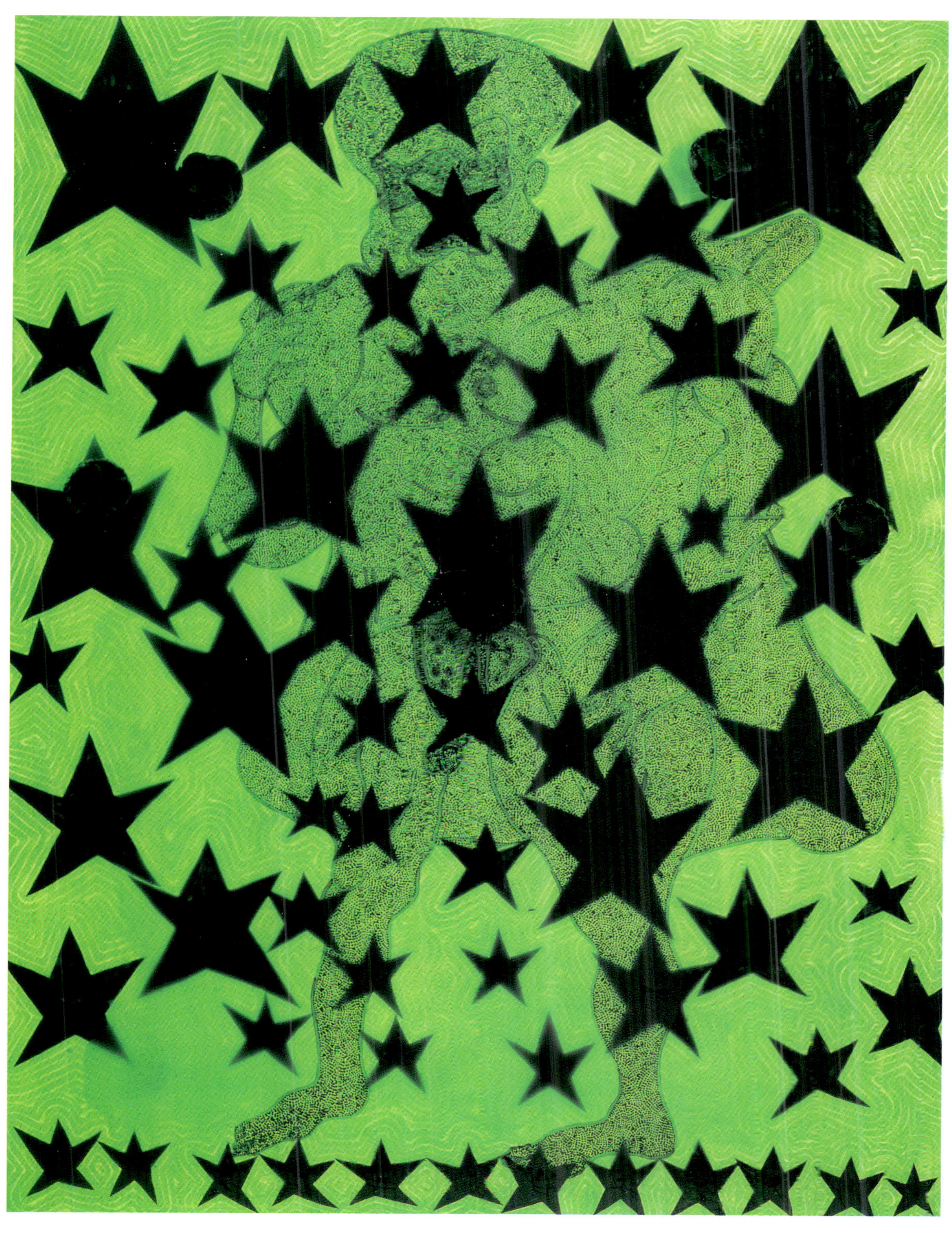

OVERLEAF: *Triple Beam Dreamer*

2001–02, acrylic, oil, leaves, glitter, polyester resin, map pins, and elephant dung on linen, with two elephant dung supports, 72 x 120 inches (182.9 x 304.8 cm)

COLLECTION OF EILEEN HARRIS NORTON, SANTA MONICA

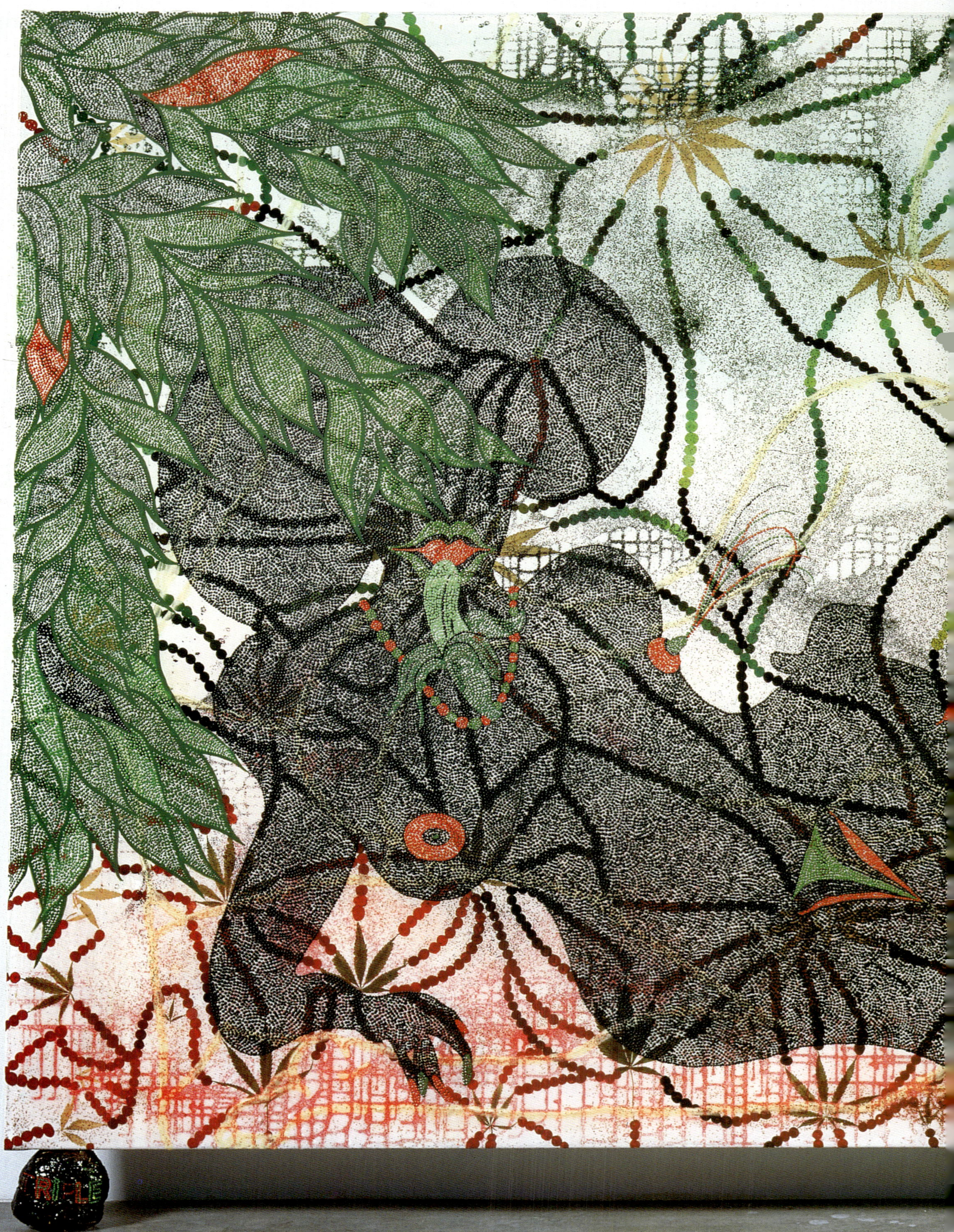
TRIPLE

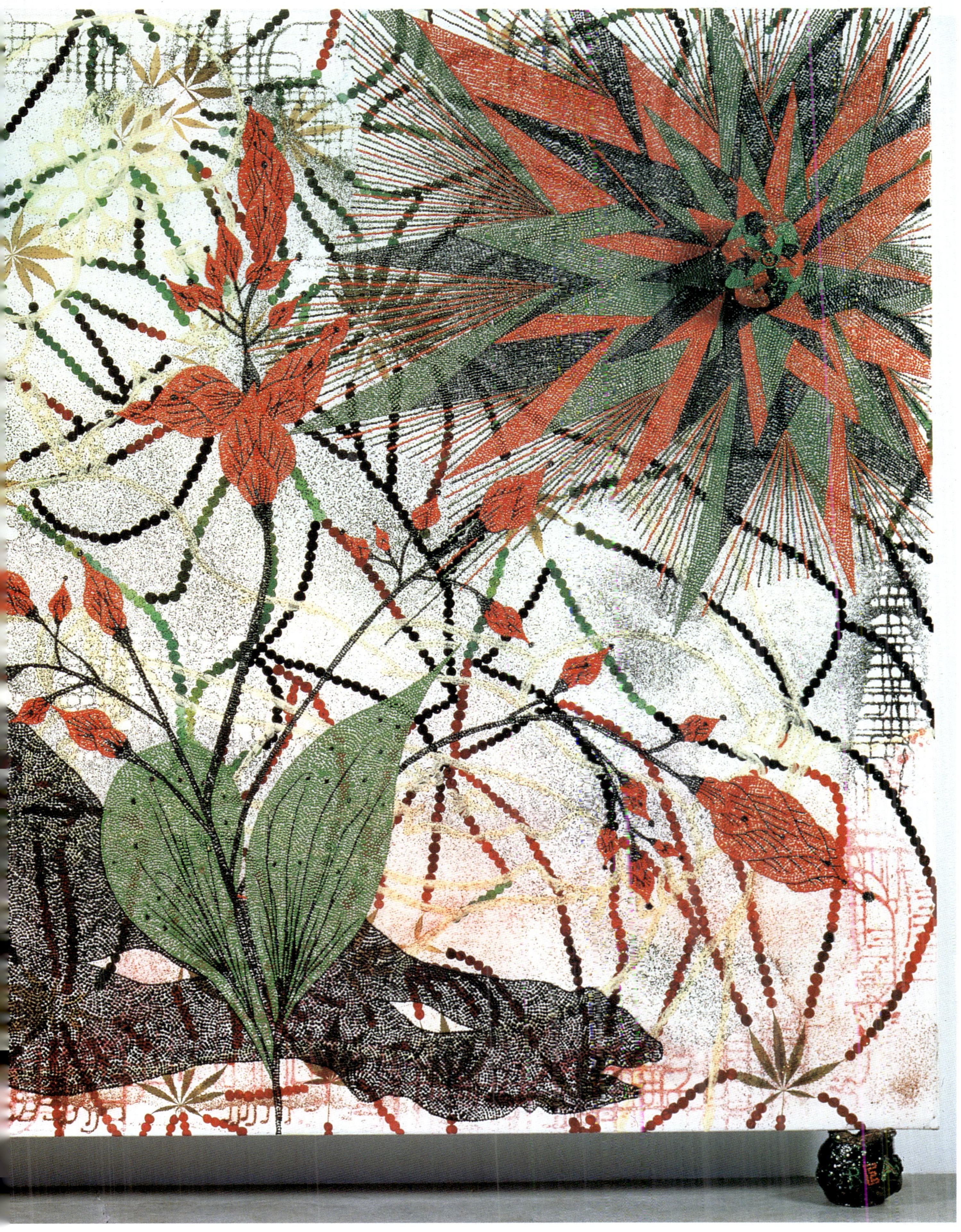

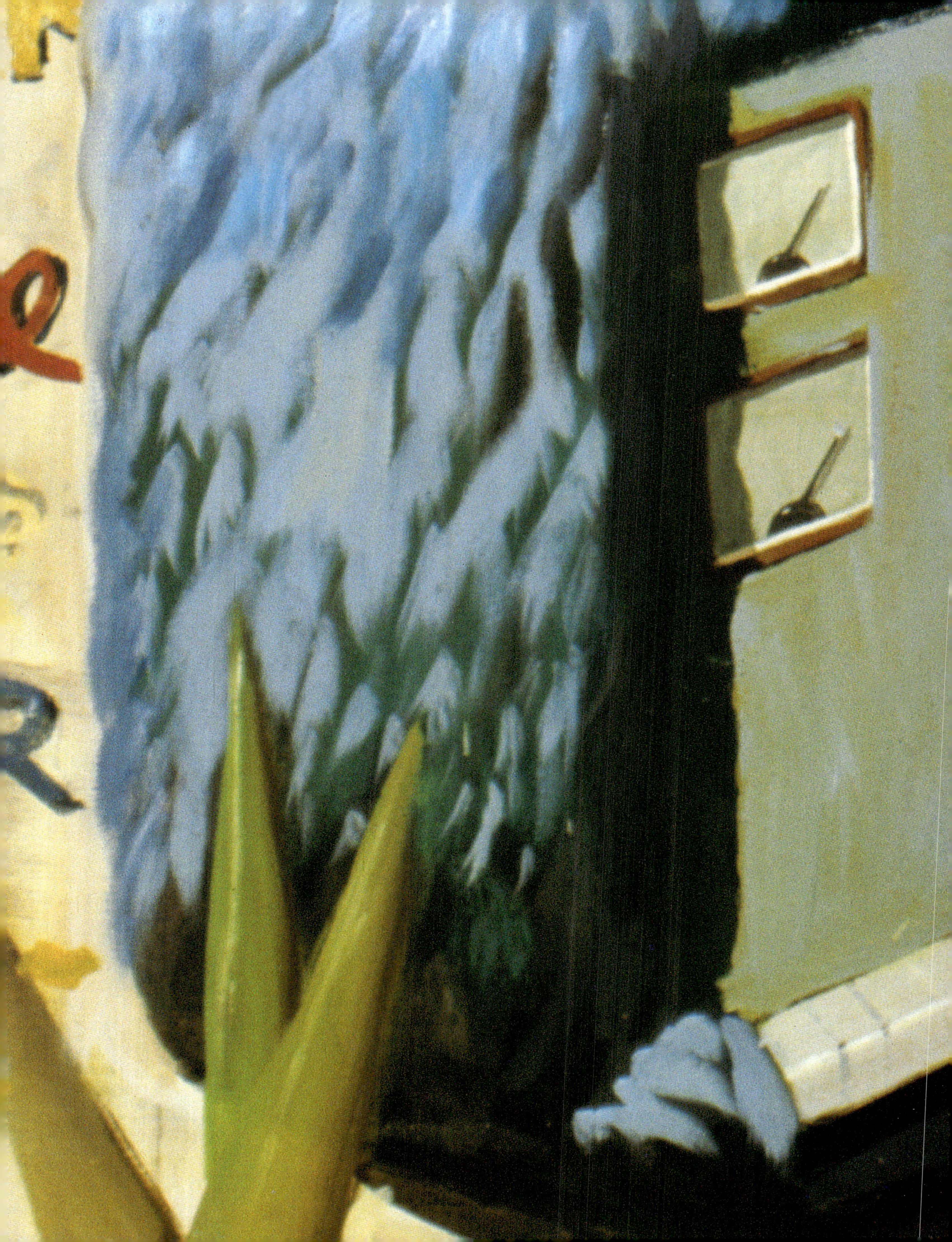

NEO RAUCH

Neid

1999, oil on canvas, 78 x 118 inches (200 x 299.8 cm)

COLLECTION OF JAY AND MARSHA SEEMAN, NEW YORK

COURTESY DAVID ZWIRNER, NEW YORK, AND GALERIE EIGEN + ART, BERLIN

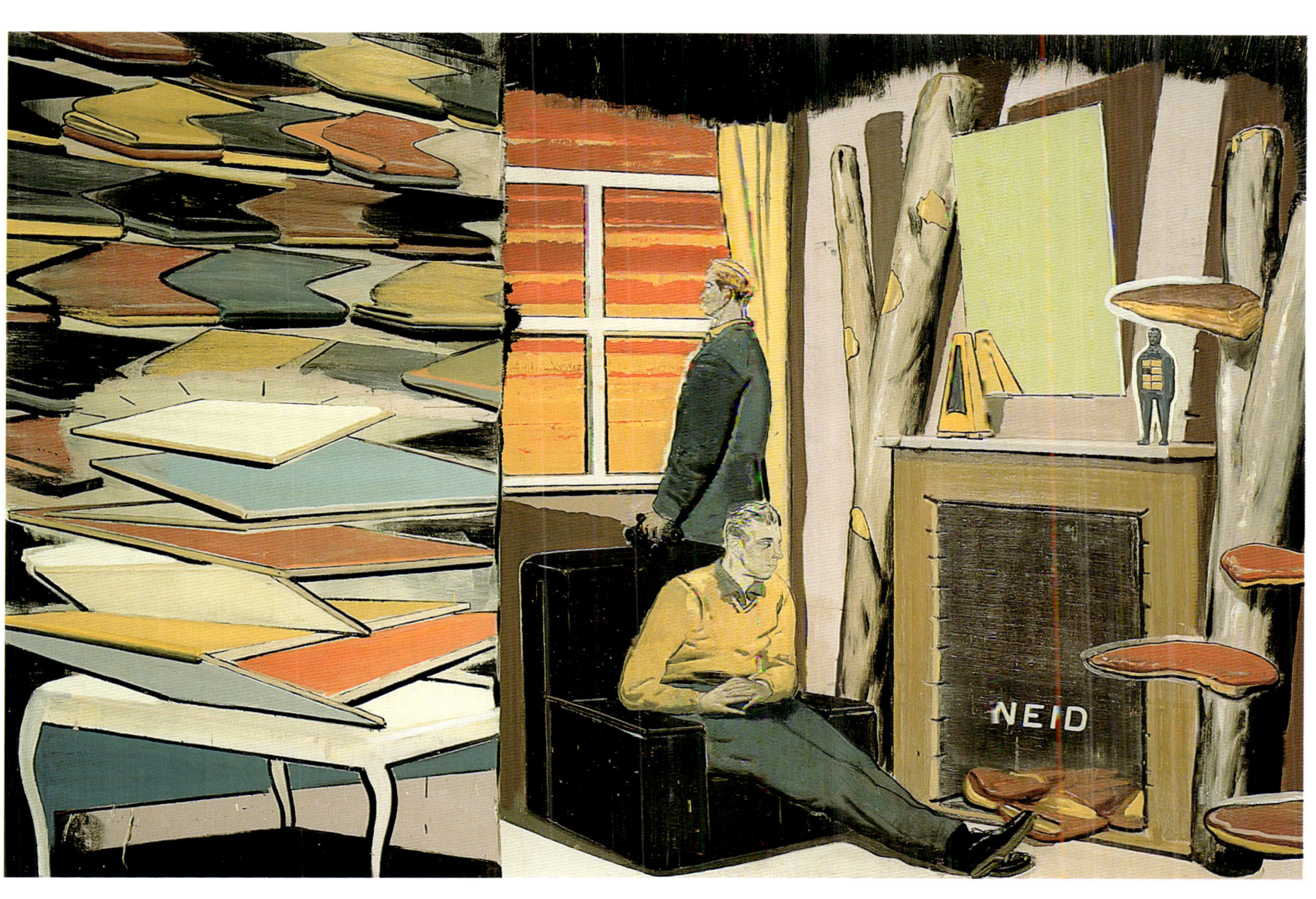
NEID

Reflex

2001, oil on canvas, 82 x 98 inches (210.2 x 250.2 cm)

COLLECTION OF DIANNE WALLACE, NEW YORK

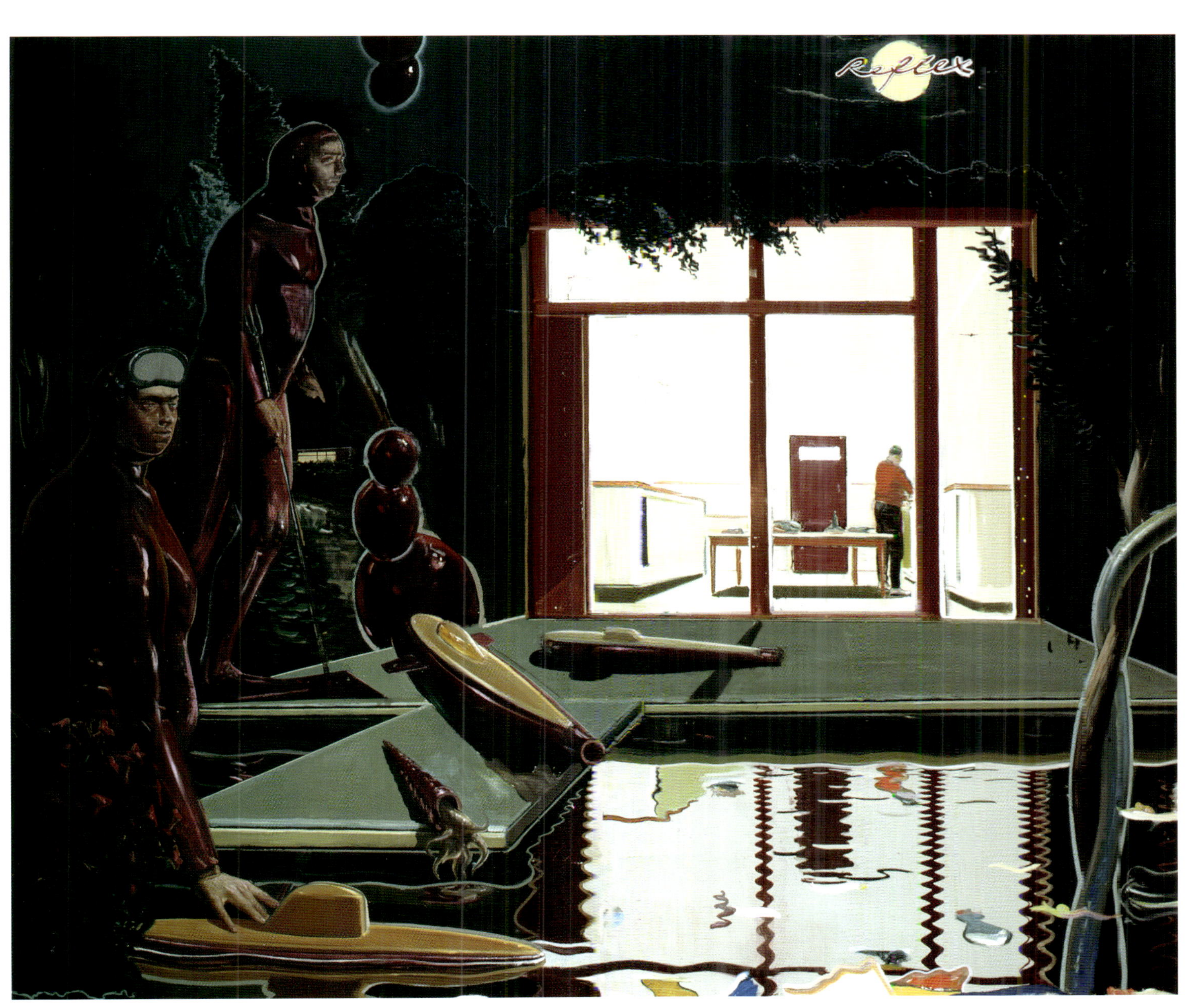
Reflex

Acker

2002, oil on canvas, 82¾ x 98½ inches (210 x 250 cm)

COLLECTION OF MELVA BUCKSBAUM AND RAYMOND J. LEARSY, NEW YORK

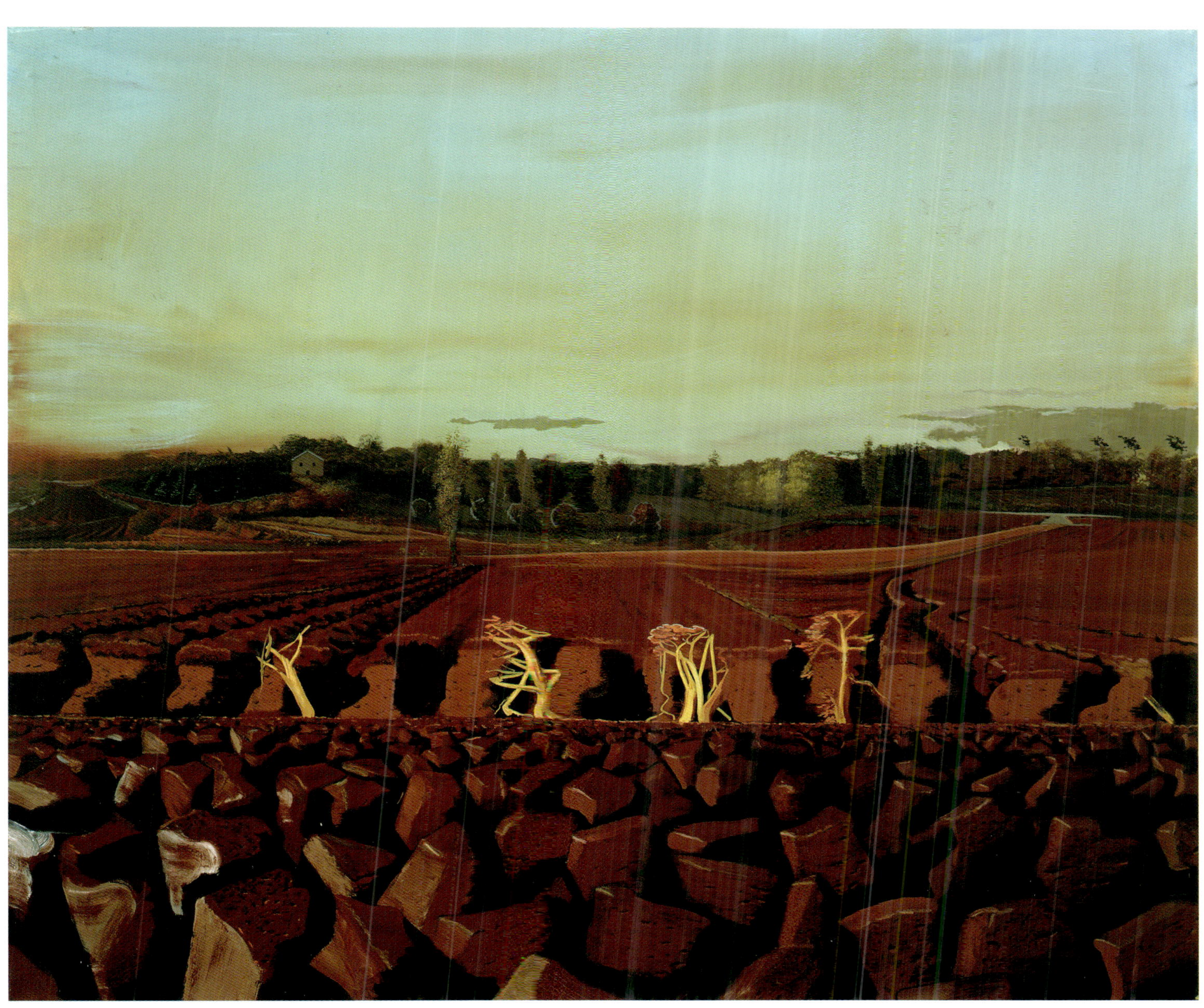

Schoepfer

2002, oil on canvas, 84 x 100 inches (213.4 x 254 cm)

PRIVATE COLLECTION, MARINA DEL REY, CALIFORNIA

COURTESY DAVID ZWIRNER, NEW YORK, AND GALERIE EIGEN + ART, BERLIN

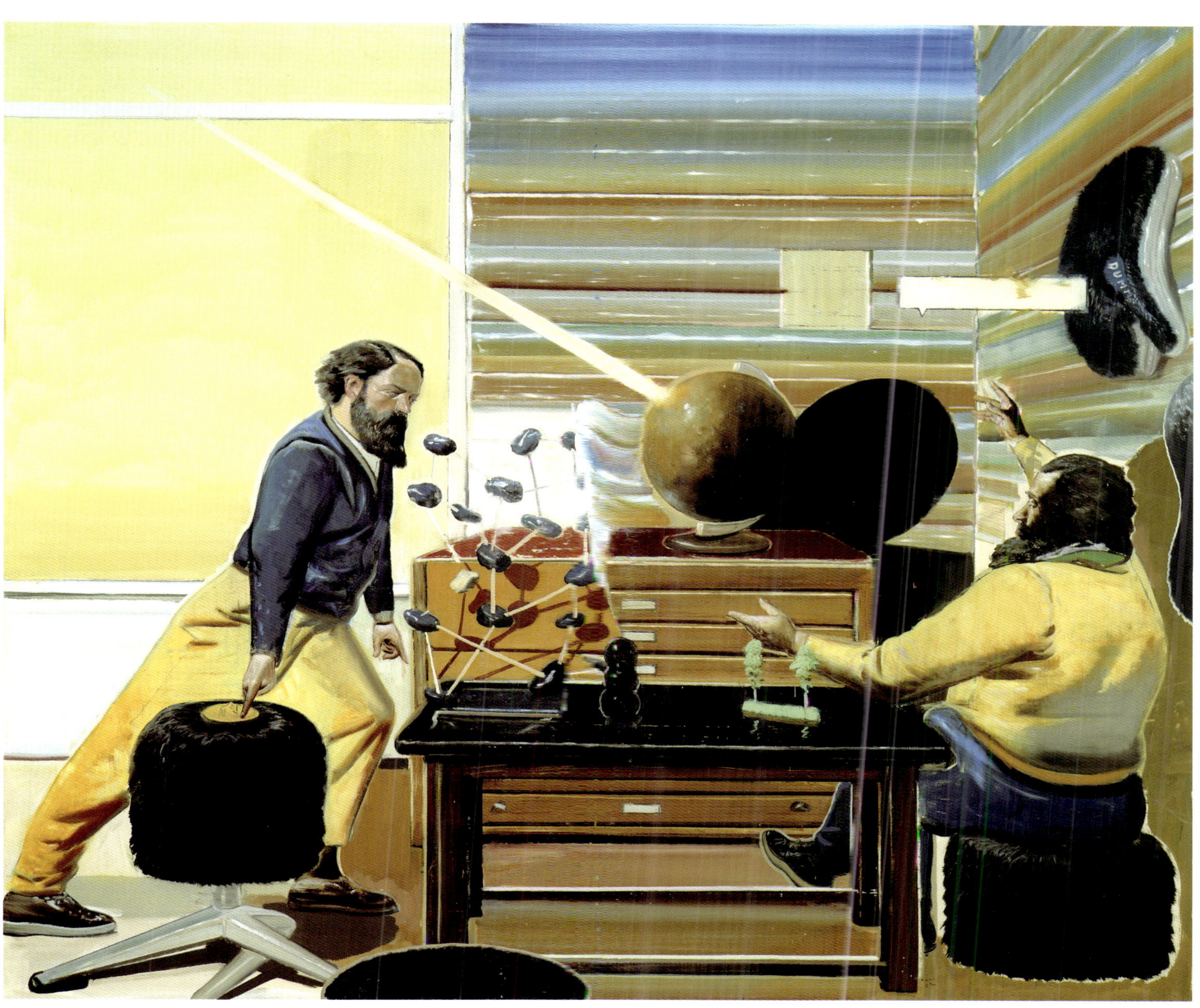

Haus des Lehrers

2003, oil on canvas, 100 x 80 inches (254 x 203.2 cm)

COLLECTION OF SUSAN AND MICHAEL HORT, NEW YORK

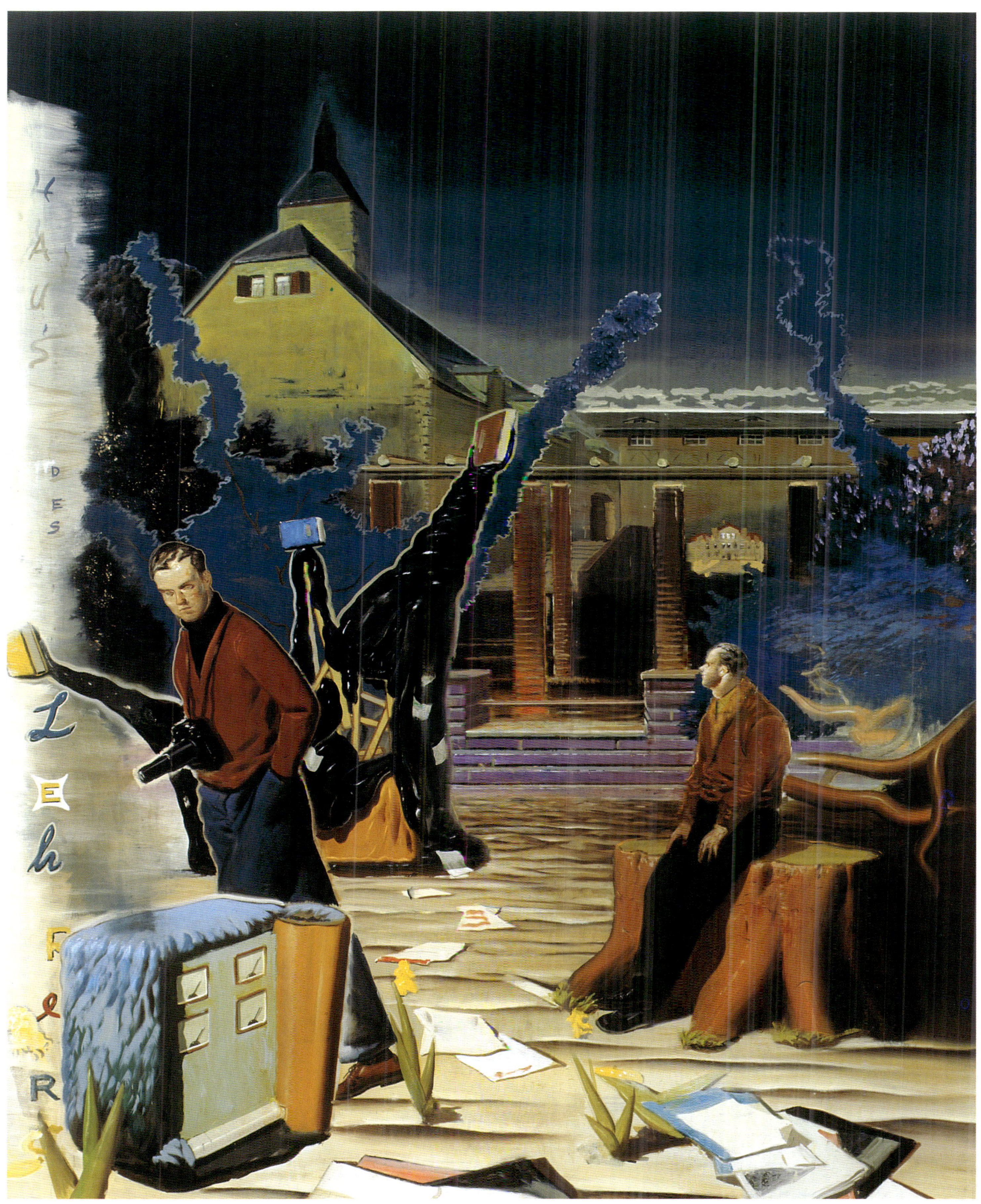
DES

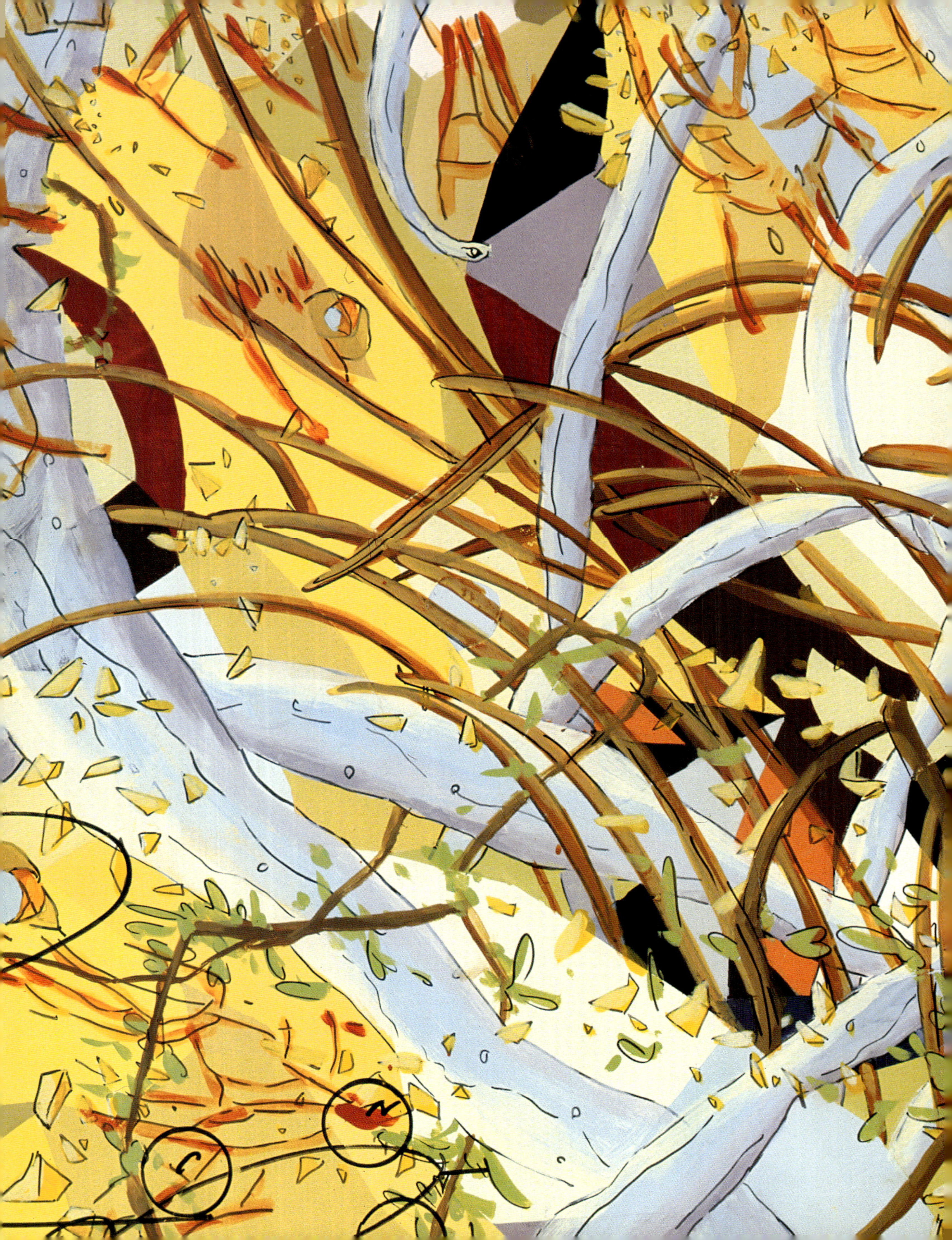

MATTHEW RITCHIE

OVERLEAF: *GNS*

Installation view, Palais de Tokyo, Paris, France, June 5–September 7, 2003

SECOND OVERLEAF: *Anti-City*

2000, oil and marker on canvas, 84 x 126 inches (213.4 x 320 cm)

THE SPEYER FAMILY COLLECTION, NEW YORK

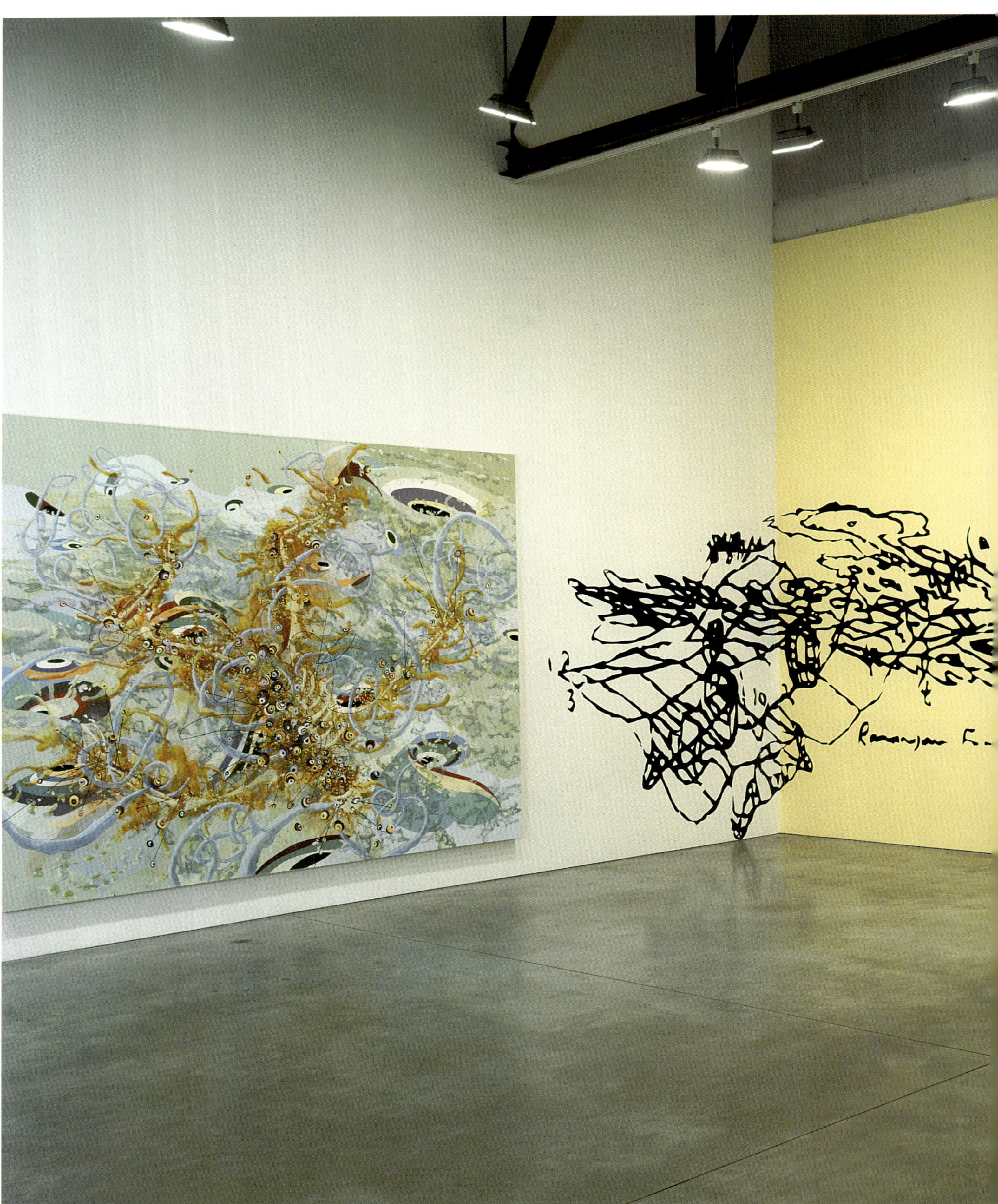

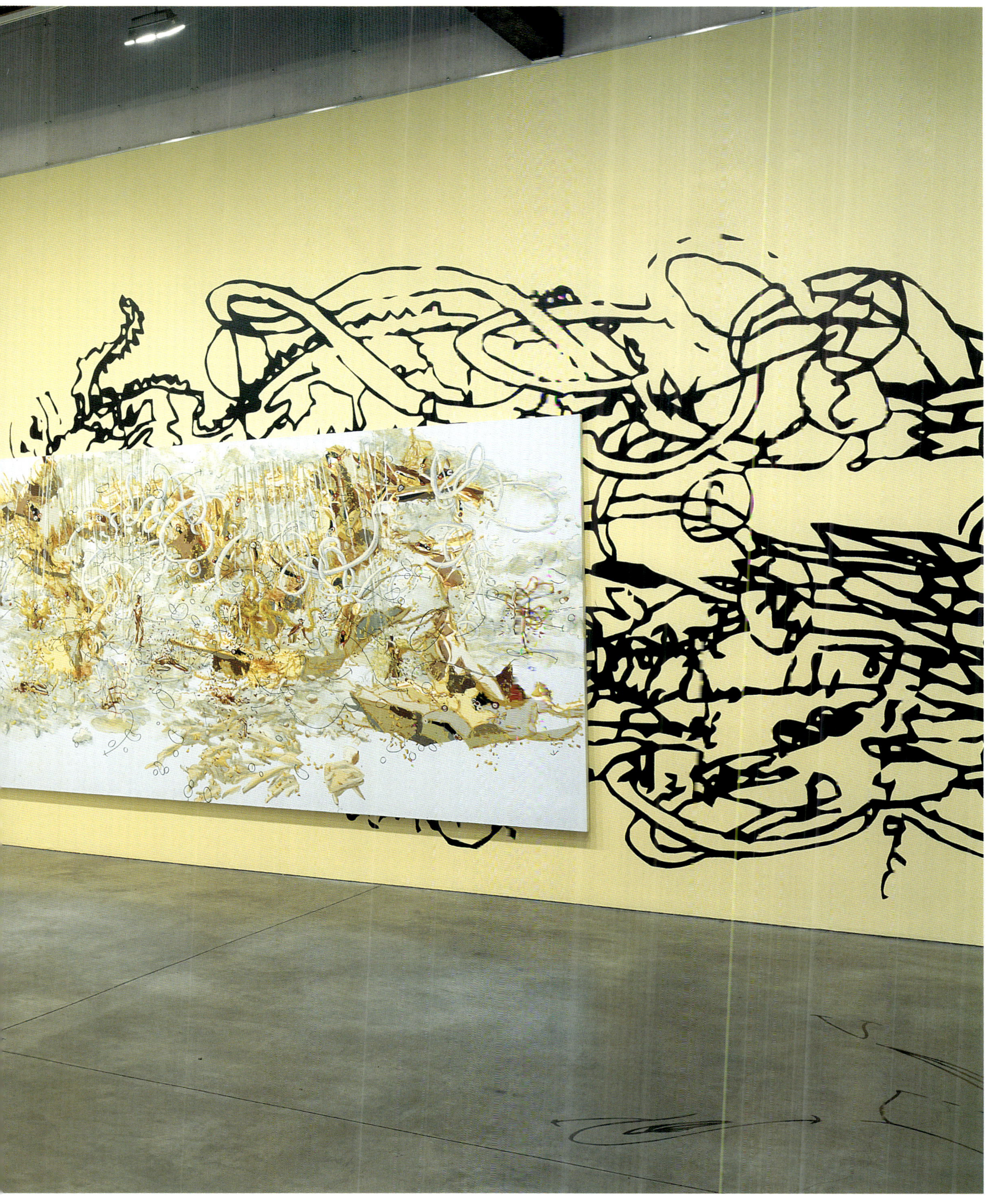

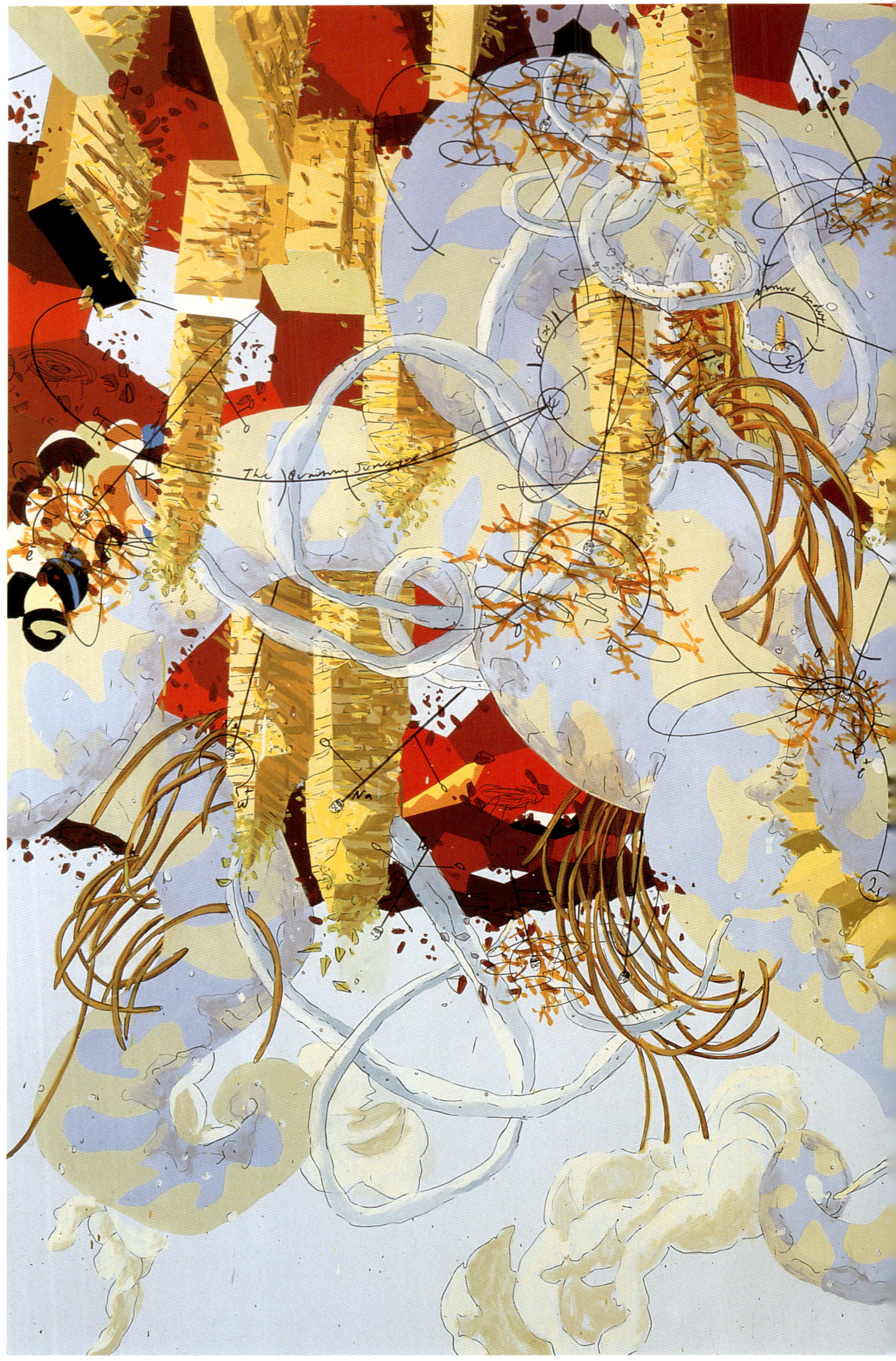

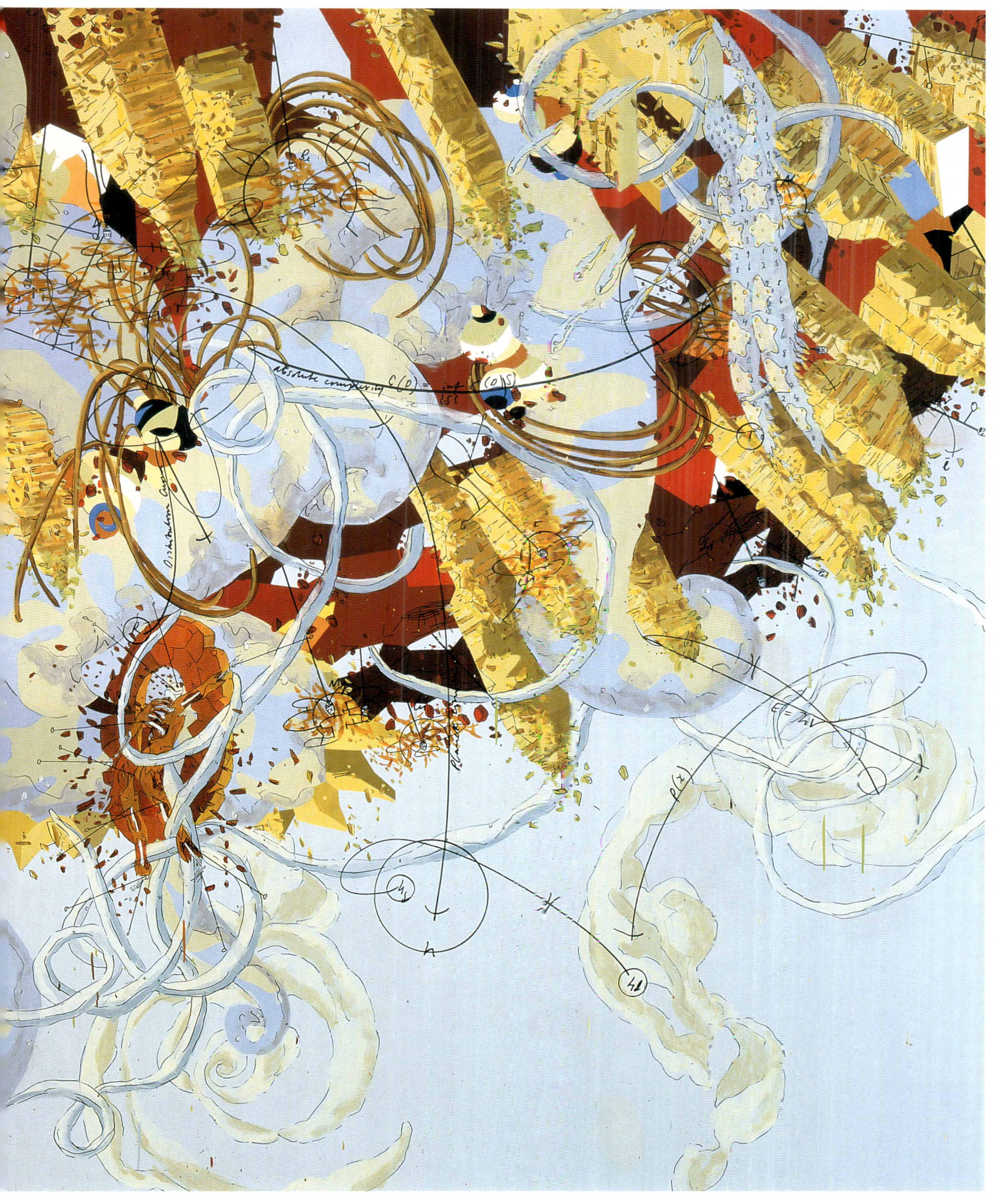

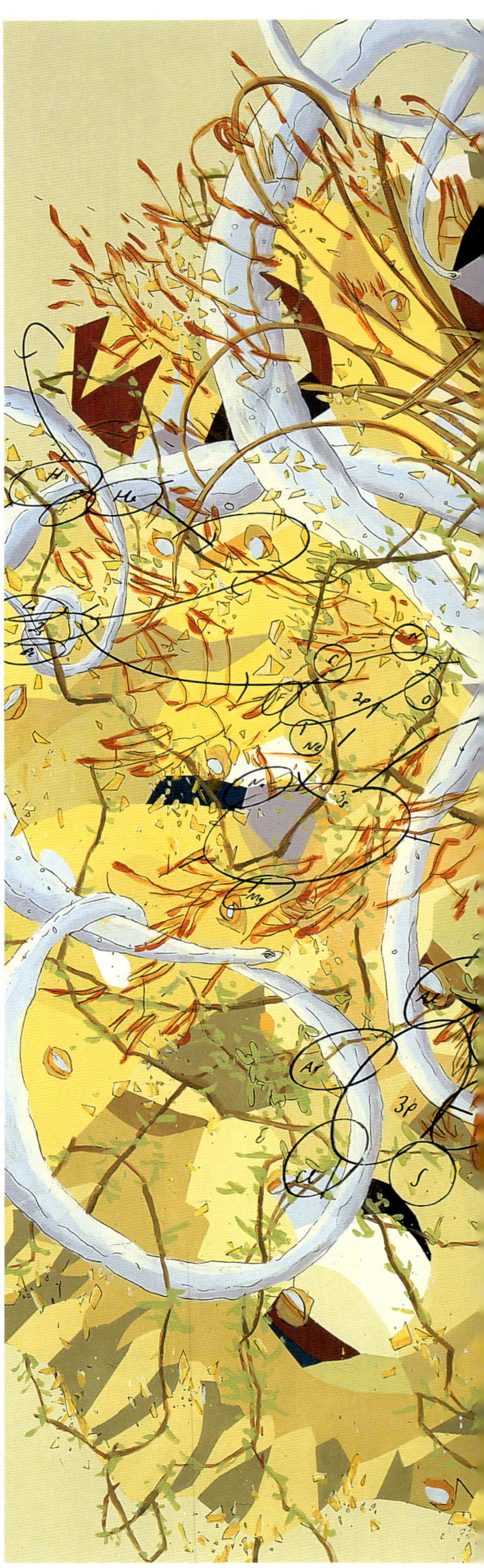

Big Top

2000, oil and marker on canvas, 84 x 96 inches (213.4 x 243.8 cm)

THE MARC AND LIVIA STRAUS FAMILY COLLECTION

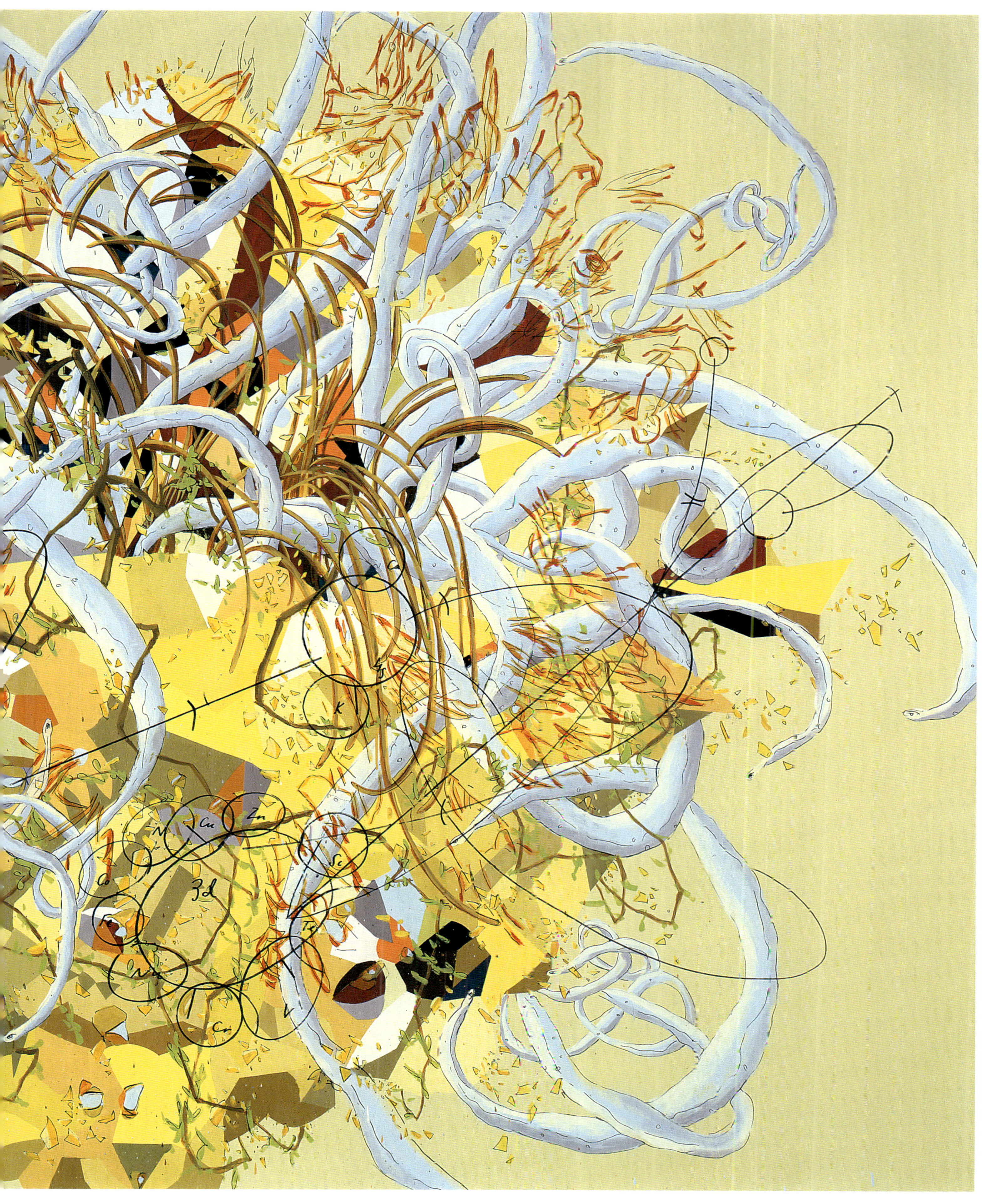

Untitled

2003, ink on denril, 12 x 48 inches (30.5 x 122 cm)

Courtesy the artist and Andrea Rosen Gallery, New York

OVERLEAF: *After Lives*

Installation view, Andrea Rosen Gallery, New York, October 19–November 23, 2002

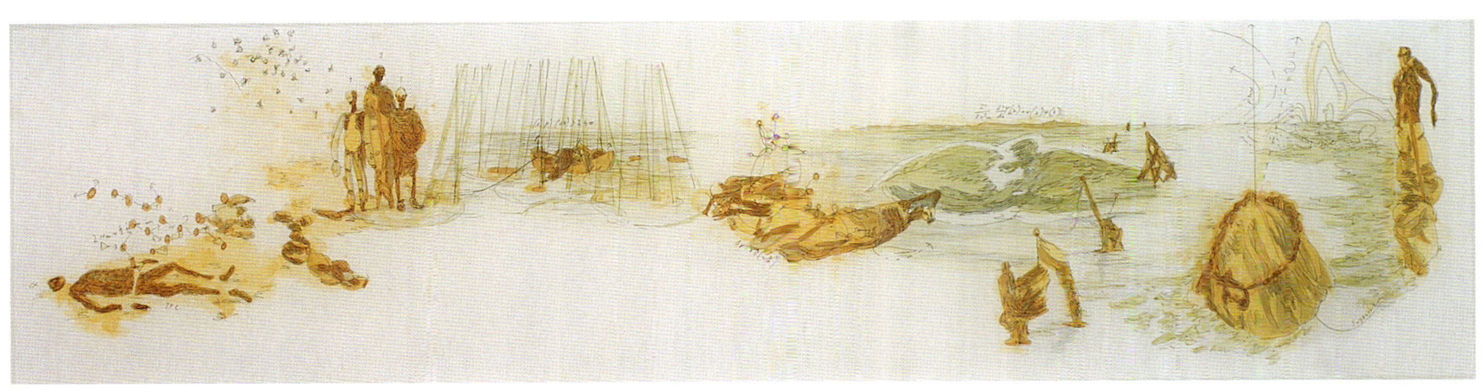

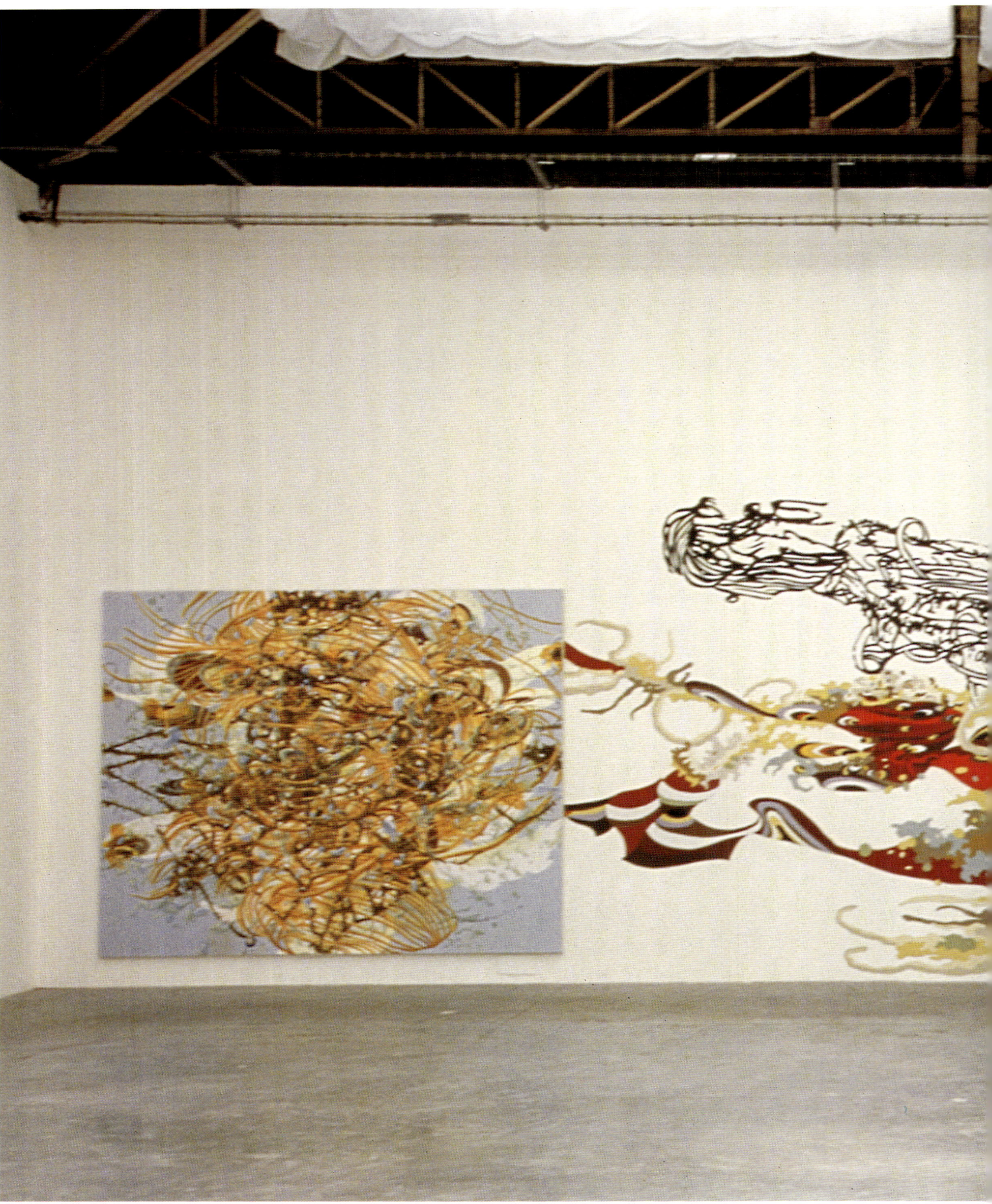

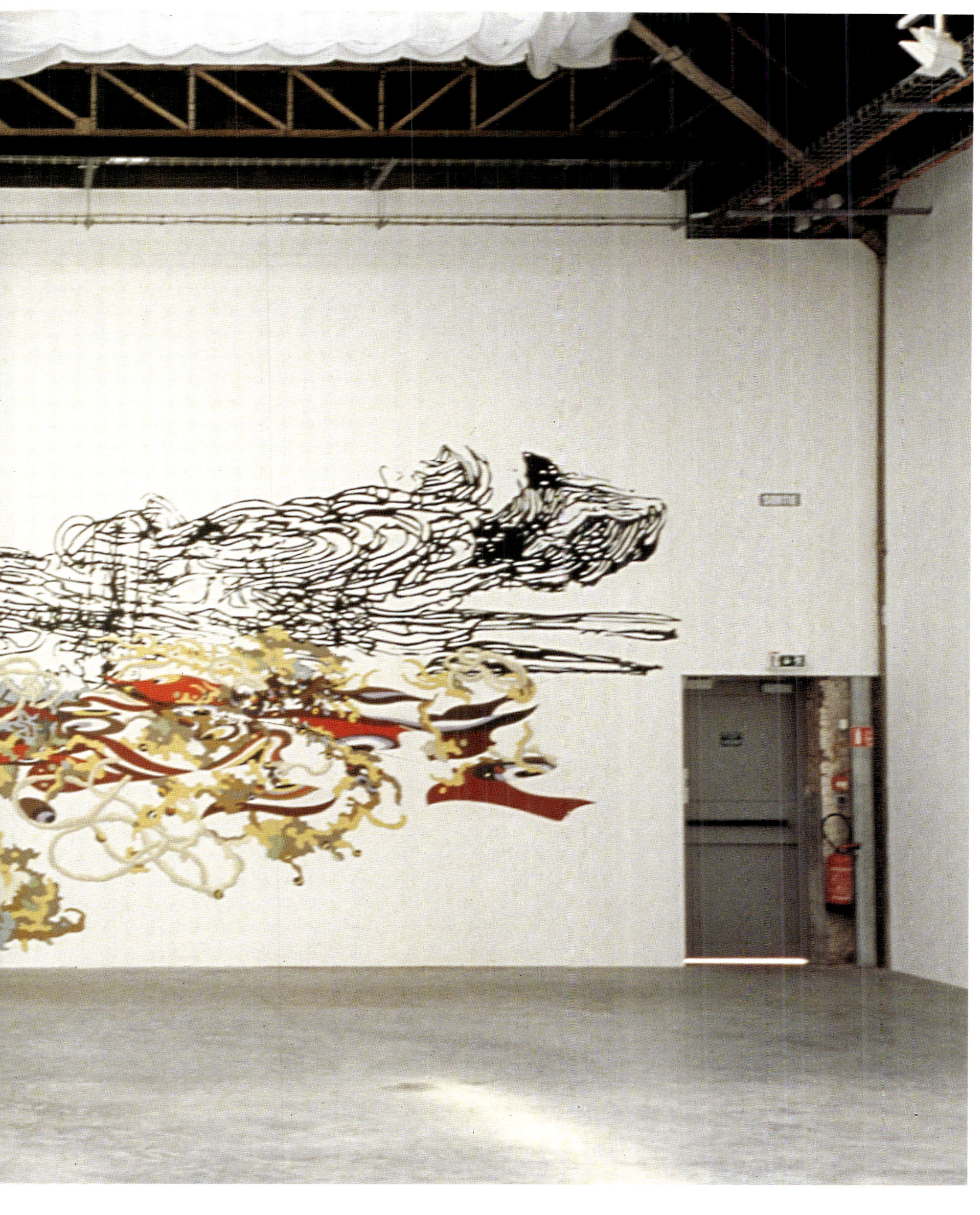

Carroll Dunham

Born in 1949, New Haven, Connecticut
Lives and works in New York City and Connecticut

EDUCATION

Trinity College, Hartford, Connecticut

SOLO EXHIBITIONS

2003 White Cube, London
Baldwin Gallery, Aspen, Colorado

2002 *Carroll Dunham*, New Museum of Contemporary Art, New York
Carroll Dunham. Drawings 1985–2002, Nolan/Eckman Gallery, New York
Drawings, Gallerie Fred Jahn, Munich, Germany
Mesokingdom, Metro Pictures, New York

2001 *The Search for Orgone*, Nolan/Eckman Gallery, New York
The Search for Orgone, c/o-Atle Gerhardsen, Berlin
Carroll Dunham, New Paintings, Gagosian Gallery, Beverly Hills, California
Carroll Dunham: Recent Prints and Related Works, Galerie Fred Jahn, Munich, Germany

2000 c/o-Atle Gerhardsen, Oslo, Norway

1999 Metro Pictures, New York
Galerie Ghislaine Hussenot, Paris
Weatherspoon Art Gallery, University of North Carolina, Greensboro, North Carolina
No Limits Events Gallery, Milan, Italy

1998 Nolan/Eckman Gallery, New York
White Cube, London
London Projects, London
c/o-Atle Gerhardsen, Oslo, Norway

1997 Metro Pictures, New York

1996 *Carroll Dunham: Paintings and Drawings 1990–1996*, Guild Hall, East Hampton, New York; traveled to: Santa Barbara Art Forum, Santa Barbara, California; Forum for Contemporary Art, St. Louis, Missouri
Nolan/Eckman Gallery, New York
Galerie Fred Jahn, Munich, Germany

1995 Bobbie Greenfield Gallery, Santa Monica, California
Carroll Dunham: Selected Paintings 1990–95, School of the Museum of Fine Arts, Boston, Massachusetts

1994 *Works on Paper*, Lemburg Gallery, Birmingham, Michigan
Sonnabend Gallery, New York

1993 Sonnabend Gallery, New York
Galerie Lehmann, Geneva, Switzerland
Nolan/Eckman Gallery, New York

1992 David Nolan Gallery, New York
Galerie Jablonka, Cologne, Germany
Carroll Dunham: Selected Paintings and Prints, Wiedner Gallery, Trinity College, Hartford, Connecticut

1991 *Carroll Dunham: Drawings*, Gallery Mukai, Tokyo
Galerie Fred Jahn, Munich, Germany

Daniel Weinberg Gallery, Santa Monica, California

1990 Sonnabend Gallery, New York

1989 Galerie Jablonka, Cologne, Germany

Sonnabend Gallery, New York

1988 *Selected Drawing,* Tyler School of Art, Temple University, Elkins Park, Pennsylvania

Drawings 1982–1983, Galerie Fred Jahn, Munich, Germany

1987 Daniel Weinberg Gallery, Los Angeles, California

Jay Gorney Modern Art, New York

1986 Barbara Krakow Gallery, Boston, Massachusetts

Baskerville & Watson Gallery, New York

1985 Daniel Weinberg Gallery, Los Angeles, California

Baskerville & Watson Gallery, New York

1981 Artists Space, New York

SELECTED GROUP EXHIBITIONS

2003 *Funny Papers,* Daniel Weinberg Gallery, Los Angeles, California

We Love Painting, Museum of Contemporary Art, Tokyo

2002 Metro Pictures, New York

Bildnis und Figur, Galerie Fred Jahn, Munich, Germany

2001 *Some Options in Abstractions,* Carpenter Center for the Visual Arts, Harvard University, Cambridge, Massachusetts

American Art, Galerie Rudolfinum, The Center of Contemporary Art, Prague, Czech Republic

2000 *End Papers,* Neuberger Museum of Art, Purchase College, State University of New York, Purchase, New York

Superorganic, Hydroponic Warfare: Carroll Dunham, David Dupuis, Alexander Ross, Derek Eller Gallery, New York

Art in America 2000, US Department of State Art in Embassies Program, Washington, D.C.

Land & Houses, Two Sequences of Drawing, Nolan/Eckman Gallery, New York

00, Barbara Gladstone Gallery, New York

Open Ends, Museum of Modern Art, New York

Olav Chr. Jensen, Sarah Morris, Carroll Dunham, c/o-Atle Gerhardsen, Berlin

1999 *Drawn by…,* Metro Pictures, New York

Art at Work: Forty Years of the Chase Manhattan Collection, Museum of Fine Arts, Houston, Texas

American Century, Part II, Whitney Museum of American Art, New York

Examining Pictures, Whitechapel Art Gallery, London; traveled to: Museum of Contemporary Art, Chicago, Illinois

1998 *Young Americans 2: New Art in the Saatchi Collection,* The Saatchi Gallery, London

Pop Surrealism, Aldrich Contemporary Art Museum, Ridgefield, Connecticut

Codex USA: Works on Paper by American Artists, Entwistle, London

Paintings: Now and Forever, Part I, Pat Hearn Gallery and Matthew Marks Gallery, New York

Art and the American Experience, Kalamazoo Institute of Arts, Kalamazoo, Michigan

1997 *Now on View,* Metro Pictures, New York

Painting Project, Basilico Fine Arts and Lehmann Maupin Gallery, New York

1996 Carpenter Center for the Visual Arts, Harvard University, Cambridge, Massachusetts

How the Chicken Crossed the Road, Mai 36 Galerie, Zurich, Switzerland

Galerie Thaddaeus Ropac, Paris

Nuevas Abstracciones, Museo Nacional Centro de Arte Reina Sofía, Madrid, Spain

1995 *1995 Biennial Exhibition,* Whitney Museum of American Art, New York

New York Abstract, Contemporary Arts Center, New Orleans, Louisiana

Carroll Dunham Lari Pittman, Jay Gorney Modern Art, New York

1994 *What's Wrong with this Picture?,* Zolla/Lieberman Gallery, Chicago, Illinois

In the Sprit of Things, Stux Gallery, New York

Dysfunction, Arthur Roger Gallery, New Orleans, Louisiana

Jay Gorney Modern Art, New York

Sonnabend Gallery, New York

1993 *Projects,* Betsy Senior Contemporary Prints, New York

What's Wrong with this Picture?, Postmasters, New York

A Series of Anniversary Exhibitions: Part II, Daniel Weinberg Gallery, Santa Monica, California

Extravagant: The Economy of Elegance, Russisches Kulturzentrum, Berlin

Drawings: 30th Anniversary Exhibition, Leo Castelli Gallery, New York

1992 *American Art of the 80s,* Museo d'Arte Moderna e Contemporanea di Trento e Rovereto, Trento, Italy

Works on Paper, David Nolan Gallery, New York

Carroll Dunham & Mel Kendrick: A Selection of Recent Work, Addison Gallery of American Art, Phillips Academy, Andover, Massachusetts

Drawn in the 90s, Katonah Museum of Art, Katonah, New York

1991 *Carroll Dunham, Mike Kelley, Cindy Sherman,* Metro Pictures, New York

Sieben Amerikanische Maler, Bayerischen Staatsgemäldesammlungen, Munich, Germany

Mel Bochner, Carroll Dunham, Barry Le Va, Galerie Faust, Geneva, Switzerland

1991 Biennial Exhibition, Whitney Museum of American Art, New York

Paintings & Drawings, Daniel Weinberg Gallery, Santa Monica, California

The Thing, Perry Rubenstein Gallery, New York

Ralph Humphrey, Matthew Weinstein, Carroll Dunham, Perry Rubenstein Gallery, New York

1990 *With the Grain: Contemporary Panel Painting,* Whitney Museum of American Art, Stamford, Connecticut, and Whitney Museum of American Art at Philip Morris, New York

Amerikanische Zeichnungen in den achtziger Jahren, Graphische Sammlung Albertina, Vienna, and Museum Morsbroich, Leverkusen, Austria

Carroll Dunham and Terry Winters, Gallery Mukai, Tokyo

Waterworks, ULAE, West Islip, New York

The Last Decade: American Artists of the 80s, Tony Shafrazi Gallery, New York

Organic Abstraction, Nelson-Atkins Museum of Art, Kansas City, Missouri

1989 *Horn of Plenty,* Stedelijk Museum, Amsterdam, The Netherlands

Wiener Diwan: Sigmund Freud-heute, Museum des 20. Jahrhunderts, Vienna, Austria

A Decade of American Drawing: 1980–1989, Daniel Weinberg Gallery, Los Angeles, California

First Impressions: Early Prints by Forty-Six Contemporary Artists, Walker Art Center, Minneapolis Minnesota

ULAE Prints, Galerie Fred Jahn, Munich, Germany

1988 *NY Art Now Part II,* Saatchi Collection, The Saatchi Gallery, London

Group Show: Carroll Dunham, Kenji Fujita, Peter Nadin, Laurie Simmons, Meyer Vaisman, Galerie Jablonka, Cologne, Germany

Vital Signs: Organic Abstraction from the Permanent Collection, Whitney Museum of American Art, New York

Altered States, Kent Fine Art, New York

1987 *Drawing Acquisitions,* Museum of Modern Art, New York

Schizophrenia, Josh Baer Gallery, New York

Coleccion Sonnabend, Museo Nacional Centro de Arte Reina Sofía, Madrid, Spain; traveled to: CAPC Musée d'Art Contemporain, Bordeaux, France; Art Cologne, Cologne, West Germany; Hamburger Bahnhof, Berlin, West Germany; Galleria Nazionale d'Arte Moderna, Rome; Museo d'Arte Moderna e Contemporanea di Trento e Roverto, Trento, Italy; Musée Rath, Geneva, Switzerland; Sezon Museum of Art, Tokyo; The Miyagi Museum of Art, Sendai, Japan; The Fukuyama Museum of Art, Fukuyama City, Japan; The National Museum of Modern Art, Kyoto, Japan

1986 *Paintings & Sculpture: Recent Acquisitions,* Museum of Modern Art, New York

Private and Public: American Prints Today, Brooklyn Museum, New York

Intuitive Line, Hirschl & Adler Modern, New York

Paravision, Margo Leavin Gallery, Los Angeles, California

Art on Paper (22nd Annual Exhibition), Weatherspoon Art Gallery, University of North Carolina, Greensboro, North Carolina

1985 *Painting as Landscape: Views of American Modernism, 1920–1984,* Parrish Art Museum, Southampton, New York; Baxter Gallery, California Institute of Technology, Pasadena, California

Currents: Carroll Dunham, Institute of Contemporary Art, Boston, Massachusetts

Group Show, International with Monument, New York

1985 Biennial Exhibition, Whitney Museum of American Art, New York

Real Surreal, Lorence Monk Gallery, New York

1984 *Brilliant Color,* Baskerville & Watson, New York

Figure in Paint, Cable Gallery, New York

New York I Dag, Nordjyllands Kunstmuseum, Aalborg, Denmark

10 Year Anniversary Exhibition, Artists Space, New York

1983 *Nine Painters,* Hallwalls, Buffalo, New York

Carroll Dunham & Terry Winters, Jan Bernier Gallery, Athens, Greece

Tradition, Transition, New Vision, Addison Gallery of American Art, Phillips Academy, Andover, Massachusetts

New Biomorphism and Automatism, Patricia Hamilton Gallery, New York

1981 *Four Painters,* Massachusetts Institute of Technology, Cambridge, Massachusetts

New Talent, New York, New Gallery, Cleveland, Ohio; Hayden Gallery, Massachusetts Institute of Technology, Cambridge, Massachusetts

1980 *Watercolors,* The Institute for Art and Urban Resources, P.S.1, Long Island City, New York

1979 *Selector's Choice,* Baltimore Museum of Art, Baltimore, Maryland

1978 *Lineup,* The Drawing Center, New York

Young American Artists, Schema Gallery, Florence, Italy

Ellen Gallagher

Born in 1965, Providence, Rhode Island

Lives and works in New York City

EDUCATION

1993 Skowhegan School of Art, Skowhegan, Maine

1992 School of the Museum of Fine Arts, Boston, Massachusetts

1989 Studio 70, Ft Thomas, Kentucky

1982–84 Oberlin College, Oberlin, Ohio

SOLO EXHIBITIONS

2003 Galerie Max Hetzler, Berlin

POMP-BANG, St. Louis Art Museum, St. Louis, Missouri

2001 *Watery Ecstatic,* Institute of Contemporary Art, Boston, Massachusetts; traveled to: Museum of Contemporary Art, Sydney, Australia

Preserve, Des Moines Art Center, Des Moines, Iowa; traveled to: Yerba Buena Center for the Arts, San Francisco; The Drawing Center, New York

Blubber, Gagosian Gallery (Chelsea), New York

2000 Anthony d'Offay Gallery, London

1999 Galerie Max Hetzler, Berlin

Mario Diacono Gallery, Boston, Massachusetts

1998 Gagosian Gallery (SoHo), New York

IKON Gallery, Birmingham, England

1996 Anthony d'Offay Gallery, London

Mary Boone Gallery, New York

1994 Mario Diacono Gallery, Boston, Massachusetts

1992 Akin Gallery, Boston, Massachusetts

SELECTED GROUP EXHIBITIONS

2003 *Black Belt,* The Studio Museum in Harlem, New York

Popstraction, Deitch Projects, New York

50th *International Art Exhibition* (directed by Francesco Bonami), *La Biennale di Venezia,* Venice, Italy

2002 *Cartoon Noir: Contemporary Investigations,* The Jack S. Blanton Museum, Austin, Texas

2001 *From Rembrandt to Rauschenberg: Building the Collection,* The Jack S. Blanton Museum of Art, Austin, Texas

The Mystery of Painting, Sammlung Goetz, Munich, Germany

The Americans, Barbican Centre, London

2000 *New Acquisitions,* Solomon R. Guggenheim Museum, New York

KIN, The Kerlin Gallery, Dublin, Ireland

Making Sense: Ellen Gallagher, Christian Marclay, Liliana Porter, Contemporary Museum, Baltimore, Maryland

Strength and Diversity: A Celebration of African American Artists, Carpenter Center for the Visual Arts, Harvard University, Cambridge, Massachusetts

American Academy Invitational Exhibition of Painting & Sculpture, American Academy of Arts and Letters, New York

Greater New York: New Art in New York Now, P.S. 1 Contemporary Art Center, Long Island City, New York

Visual Memoirs: Selected Paintings and Drawings, Brandeis University, Waltham, Massachusetts

1999 *(Corps) Social,* École Nationale Supérieure des Beaux-Arts, Paris

Negotiating Small Truths, The Jack S. Blanton Museum of Art, Austin, Texas

Collectors Collect Contemporary: 1990–99, Institute of Contemporary Art, Boston, Massachusetts

1998 *Cinco Continentes y una Ciudad,* Museo de la Ciudad de Mexico, Mexico City

Postcards from Black America, De Beyerd Centre for Contemporary Art, Breda, The Netherlands

Piecing Together the Puzzle: Recent Acquisitions, Museum of Modern Art, New York

1997 *Project Painting,* Basilico Fine Arts and Lehmann Maupin Gallery, New York

Projects, Irish Museum of Modern Art, Dublin, Ireland

The Body of Painting, Mario Diacono Gallery, Boston, Massachusetts

T-Race, Randolph Street Gallery, London

1996 *Art at the End of the 20th Century: Selections from the Whitney Museum of American Art,* National Art Gallery and Alexandros Soutzos Museum, Athens, Greece; traveled to: Museu d'Art Contemporani, Barcelona, Spain; Kunstmuseum Bonn, Bonn, Germany; Castello di Rivoli, Turin, Italy

Inside the Visible, Institute of Contemporary Art, Boston, Massachusetts, and Whitechapel Gallery, London

1995 *1995 Biennial Exhibition,* Whitney Museum of American Art, New York

Altered States, Forum for Contemporary Art, St. Louis, Missouri

Degrees of Abstractions, Museum of Fine Arts, Boston, Massachusetts

1994 *Airbourne/Earthbound,* Mario Diacono Gallery, Boston, Massachusetts

In Context, Institute of Contemporary Art, Boston, Massachusetts

1993 *Artists Select,* Artists Space, New York

Traveling Scholar's Exhibit, Museum of Fine Arts, Boston, Massachusetts

Chris Ofili

Born in 1968, Manchester, England
Lives and works in London

EDUCATION

1992 Exchange to Hochschule der Künste, Berlin
1991–93 MA Fine Art, Royal College of Art, London
1988–91 BA Fine Art, Chelsea School of Art, London
1987–88 Foundation Course, Thameside College of Technology, Ashton-u-Lyme, England

SOLO EXHIBITIONS

2003 *Within Reach*, British Pavilion, *La Biennale di Venezia*, Venice, Italy
2002 *Freedom One Day*, Victoria Miro Gallery, London
2001 *Chris Ofili Water-colours*, Gallery Side 2, Tokyo
2000 *Chris Ofili Drawings*, Victoria Miro Gallery, London
1999 Le Case d'Arte, Milan
Afrobiotics, Gavin Brown's enterprise, New York
1998 Whitworth Art Gallery, Manchester, England
Southampton City Art Gallery, Southampton, England
Serpentine Gallery, London
1997 *Pimpin ain't easy but it sure is fun*, Contemporary Fine Arts, Berlin
1996 *Afrodizzia*, Victoria Miro Gallery, London
1995 Gavin Brown's enterprise, New York
1991 *Paintings and Drawings*, Kepler Gallery, London

SELECTED GROUP EXHIBITIONS

2002 *Cavepainting*, Santa Monica Museum of Art, Santa Monica, California
Life is Beautiful, Laing Art Gallery, Newcastle upon Tyne, England
Drawing Now: Eight Propositions, MoMA QNS, Queens, New York
2001 *Public Offerings*, Museum of Contemporary Art, Los Angeles, California
Works on Paper from Acconci to Zittel, Victoria Miro Gallery, London
Form Follows Fiction, Castello di Rivoli, Turin, Italy
One Planet under a Groove: Hip Hop and Contemporary Art, Bronx Museum of the Arts, New York; traveled to Walker Art Center, Minneapolis, Minnesota; Spelman College Museum of Fine Art, Atlanta, Georgia
2000 *Raw*, Victoria Miro Gallery, London
Sydney Bienniale, Museum of Contemporary Art, Sydney, Australia
Ant Noises 1, The Saatchi Gallery, London
1999 *History of the Turner Prize*, ArtSway, Hampshire, England
Trouble Spot Painting, NICC and MUHKA, Antwerp, The Netherlands
6th International Istanbul Biennial, Istanbul, Turkey
Carnegie International, Carnegie Museum of Art, Pittsburgh, Pennsylvania
Sensation. Young British Artists From The Saatchi Collection, Brooklyn Museum, Brooklyn, New York
1998 *A to Z*, The Approach, London
Heads will roll, Victoria Miro Gallery, London
The Jerwood Foundation Painting Prize, Jerwood Gallery, London
The Turner Prize, Tate Gallery, London

1997 *Date with an artist,* Northern Gallery for Contemporary Art, Sunderland, England

Popoccultural, curated by Cabinet Gallery, Southampton City Gallery, Southampton, England

Belladonna, Institute of Contemporary Arts, London

Pictura Britannica, Museum of Contemporary Art, Sydney, Australia; traveled to: Art Gallery of Australia, Adelaide, Australia; Museum of New Zealand Te Papa Tongarewa, Wellington, New Zealand

Sensation. Young British Artists from the Saatchi Collection, Royal Academy of Arts, London

Minor Sensation, Victoria Miro Gallery, London

20th John Moore's Liverpool Exhibition of Contemporary Painting, Walker Art Gallery, Liverpool, England

1996 *Mothership Connection,* Stedelijk Museum Bureau, Amsterdam, The Netherlands

About Vision: New British Painting in the 1990s, Museum of Modern Art, Oxford, England; traveled to: Christchurch Mansion, Ipswich, England; The Fruitmarket Gallery, Edinburgh, Scotland; Laing Art Gallery, Newcastle upon Tyne, England

Young British Artists, Roslyn Oxley9 Gallery, Paddington, Australia

NowHere, Louisiana Museum of Modern Art, Louisiana, Denmark

Maps Elsewhere, Institute of International Visual Arts, London

Popoccultura, curated by Cabinet Gallery, South London Gallery, London

1995 *Cocaine Orgasm,* Bank Space, London

Im/Pure, Osterwalder's Art Office, Hamburg, Germany

John Moore's Exhibition, Walker Art Gallery, Liverpool, England

Contained, Cultural Instructions, London

A Bonnie Situation, Contemporary Fine Art, Berlin

Brilliant! New Art from London, Walker Art Center, Minneapolis, Minnesota; traveled to: Contemporary Arts Museum, Houston, Texas

Selections Spring '95, The Drawing Center, New York

1994 *Take Five,* Anthony Wilkinson Fine Art, London

Painting Show, Victoria Miro Gallery, London

1993 *BT New Contemporaries,* Cornerhouse Gallery, Manchester, England; traveled to: Orchard Gallery, Derry, Ireland; Mappin Art Gallery, Sheffield, England; Stoke-on-Trent Gallery; CCA, Glasgow, Scotland

Shit Sale, Brick Lane, London

Shit Sale, Strasse 17 Juni, Berlin

Borderless Print, Rochdale Art Gallery, London

To Boldly Go, Cubitt Street Gallery, London

Riverside Open, Riverside Gallery, London

Lift, Atlantis Basement, London

1992 Pachipamwe International artists' workshop exhibition, Bulawayo Art Gallery, Harare, Zimbabwe

1991 *Whitworth Young Contemporaries,* Whitworth Art Gallery, Manchester, England

BP Portrait Award, National Portrait Gallery, London

Blauer Montag, Raum für Kunst, Basel, Switzerland

1990 *Whitworth Young Contemporaries,* Whitworth Art Gallery, Manchester, England

BP Portrait Award, National Portrait Gallery, London

1989 *Whitworth Young Contemporaries,* Whitworth Art Gallery, Manchester, England

Neo Rauch

Born in 1960, Leipzig, Germany
Lives and works in Leipzig

EDUCATION

1993–98 Assistant, Hochschule für Grafik und Buchkunst, Leipzig, Germany
1986–90 Master student with Professor Bernhard Heisig
1981–86 Studied at the Hochschule für Grafik und Buchkunst, Leipzig, Germany

SOLO EXHIBITIONS

2002 David Zwirner, New York
Neo Rauch, Bonnefantenmuseum, Maastricht, The Netherlands

2001 *Randgebiet,* Haus der Kunst, Munich, Germany
Randgebiet, Kunsthalle Zurich, Zurich, Switzerland
International Culture Centre, Krakow, Poland

2000 Galerie EIGEN + ART, Leipzig, Germany
David Zwirner, New York

1998 Galerie EIGEN + ART, Berlin
Galerie der Stadt Backnang, Backnang, Germany

1997 *Manöver,* Galerie EIGEN + ART, Leipzig, Germany
Museum der bildenden Künste, Leipzig, Germany

1995 Dresdner Bank, Leipzig, Germany
Galerie EIGEN + ART, Berlin
Marineschule, Overbeck Gesellschaft, Lübeck, Germany

1994 Projektgalerie, Kunstverein Elsterpark e.V., Leipzig, Germany

1993 Galerie Alvensleben, Munich, Germany
Galerie VOXX, Chemnitz, Germany
Galerie EIGEN + ART, Leipzig, Germany
ImkabinettGalerie, Berlin
Galerie Schwind, Frankfurt am Main, Germany

1989 Galerie am Thomaskirchhof, Leipzig, Germany

SELECTED GROUP EXHIBITIONS

2003 *For the Record: Drawing Contemporary Life,* Vancouver Art Gallery, Vancouver, British Columbia

Social Strategies: Redefining Social Realism, University Art Museum, University of California Santa Barbara, Santa Barbara, California; traveled to: University Galleries, Illinois State University, Normal, Illinois; DePauw University Art Gallery, Greencastle, Indiana

2002 *Drawing Now: Eight Propositions,* Museum of Modern Art, New York

Dear Painter, Paint Me, Centre Georges Pompidou, Paris; traveled to: Kunsthalle Wien, Vienna, Austria; Schrin Kunsthalle Frankfurt, Germany

Pertaining to Painting Contemporary Arts Museum, Houston, Texas; traveled to: Austin Museum of Art, Austin, Texas

2001 *49th International Art Exhibition, La Biennale di Venezia*, Venice, Italy
EU, Stephen Friedman Gallery, London
I ♥ NY, David Zwirner, New York
The Mystery of Painting, Sammlung Goetz, Munich, Germany

2000 *Premio Michetti*, Museo Michetti, Francavilla al Mare, Italy

1999 *After the Wall,* Moderna Museet, Stockholm, Sweden

Children of Berlin, P.S. 1 Contemporary Art Center, Long Island City, New York

Drawing and Painting, Galerie EIGEN + ART, Berlin

German Open, Kunstmuseum Wolfsburg, Wolfsburg, Germany

Malerei, INIT Kunsthalle, Berlin

The Golden Age, Institute of Contemporary Arts, London

1998 *Die Macht des Alters—Strategien der Meisterschaft,* Deutsches Historisches Museum Berlin, Berlin; traveled to: Kunstmuseum Bonn, Bonn, Germany; Deutsches Hygiene Museum, Dresden, Germany

Transmission, Espace des Arts, Chalon-sur-Saône, France

1997 *Figural. Figürlich. Figurativ.,* Bankhaus Trinkhaus & Burkhardt, Düsseldorf, Germany

Group Show, Galerie EIGEN + ART, Berlin

Lust und Last, Germanisches Nationalmuseum, Nürnberg, Germany; traveled to: Museum der Bildenden Künste, Leipzig, Germany

Need for Speed, Grazer Kunstverein, Graz, Austria

1996 *Der Blick ins 21ste,* Kunstverein Düsseldorf, Düsseldorf, Germany

1995 Goethe House (with Maren Roloff), New York

1994 1. Saechsische Kunstausstellung, Dresden, Germany

1993 *Künstler träumen Berlin,* Marstall, Berlin

1992 *Der Harz*, Galerie am Kraftwerk/ Dependance Specks Hof, Leipzig, Germany

Galerie Alvensleben, Munich, Germany

Leipziger Sezession, Krochhochhaus, Leipzig, Germany

Junge Künstler aus Leipzig, BASF, Ludwigshafen, Germany

RENTA Preis, Norris Halle, Nürnberg, Germany

Reflex Ost-West, Potsdam, Germany

1991 *Das Gewitter* (with Klaus Killich), Galerie am Kraftwerk Leipzig, Germany

1990 Galerie Maerz (with Roland Borchers and Gerhard Petri), Linz, Austria

1989 *Große Kunstausstellung NRW*, Düsseldorf, Germany

Zwischenspiele, Künstlerhaus Bethanien, Berlin, West Germany

Junge Künstler der DDR und Kubas, Berlin, East Germany; traveled to: Havanna, Cuba

1988 *X. Kunstausstellung der DDR*, Dresden, Germany

Arbeiten aus vier Kunsthochschulen Leipzig, Warsaw, Vienna, Berlin, Hofer Gesellschaft, Bahnhof Westend, Berlin, West Germany

Neuerwerbungen des Ludwig-Institut für Kunst der DDR, Ludwig-Institut, Oberhausen, Germany

Matthew Ritchie

Born in 1964, London, England
Lives and works in New York City

EDUCATION

1983–86 BFA, Camberwell School of Art, London
1982 Boston University, Boston, Massachusetts

SOLO EXHIBITIONS

2004 Mass MoCA, North Adams, Massachusetts
2003 *After the Father Costume,* c/o-Atle Gerhardsen, Berlin, Germany
Proposition: Player, Contemporary Arts Museum, Houston, Texas
2002 *After Lives,* Andrea Rosen Gallery, New York
2001 *Concentrations 38: Matthew Ritchie,* Dallas Museum of Art, Dallas, Texas
The Family Farm, White Cube, London
2000 *Parents and Children,* Andrea Rosen Gallery, New York
The Fast Set, Museum of Contemporary Art, North Miami, Florida
1999 c/o-Atle Gerhardsen, Oslo, Norway
The Big Story, Cleveland Center for Contemporary Art, Cleveland, Ohio
1998 Fundação Cultural do Distrito Federal, Brasília, Brazil
Paco Imperial, Rio de Janeiro, Brazil
Galeria Camargo Vilaca, São Paolo, Brazil
The Gamblers, Basilico Fine Arts, New York
Mario Diacono Gallery, Boston, Massachusetts
1997 *Omniverse,* Nexus Contemporary Art Center, Atlanta, Georgia
Mario Diacono Gallery, Boston, Massachusetts
1996 *The Hard Way, Chapter III,* c/o-Atle Gerhardsen, Oslo, Norway
The Hard Way, Chapter II, Basilico Fine Arts, New York
The Hard Way, Chapter I, Galerie Meteo, Paris
1995 *working model,* Basilico Fine Arts, New York

SELECTED GROUP EXHIBITIONS

2003 *GNS,* Palais de Tokyo, Paris
Painting Pictures, Kunstmuseum Wolfsburg, Wolfsburg, Germany
Journey to Now, Art Gallery of South Australia, John Kaldor Art Projects and Collection, Adelaide, Australia
2002 *Reverberator,* Houldsworth Gallery, London
(The World May Be) Fantastic, Biennale of Sydney 2002, Sydney, Australia
Flights of Reality, Kettle's Yard, University of Cambridge, Cambridge, England; traveled to: The Turnpike Gallery, Greater Manchester, England
Sprawl, Contemporary Arts Center, Cincinnati, Ohio
Urgent Painting, LARC/Musée d'Art Moderne, Paris
Once Upon a Time, New York State Museum, Albany, New York
Drawing Now: Eight Propositions, MoMA QNS, Queens, New York
Virginie Barré + Christophe Berdaguer & Marie Péjus + Alain Declercq + Michael Elmgreen & Ingar Dragset + Naomi Fisher + Gelatin + Subodh Gupta + Alexander Györfi + Kay Hassan + Gunilla

Klingberg + Surasi Kusolwong + Michel Majerus + Paola Pivi + Matthew Ritchie + Franck Scurti + Wang-Du + Sislej Xhafa + Jun'ya Yamaide, Palais de Tokyo, Paris

2001 *Form Follows Fiction,* Castello di Rivoli, Turin, Italy

New Acquisitions from the Dakis Joannou Collection, Centre for Contemporary Art, Athens, Greece

All Systems Go, Contemporary Arts Museum, Houston, Texas

Selections from the Permanent Collection, Museum of Contemporary Art, North Miami, Florida

Collaborations with Parkett: 1984–Now, Museum of Modern Art, New York

010101: Art in Technological Times, San Francisco Museum of Modern Art, San Francisco, California

futureland2001.com, Museum van Bommel van Dam, Venlo, The Netherlands

The World According to the Newest and Most Exact Observations: Mapping Art and Science, The Tang Teaching Museum and Art Gallery, Skidmore College, Saratoga Springs, New York

futureland2001.com, Städtisches Museum Abteiberg, Mönchengladbach, Germany

2000 *Faith,* Aldrich Contemporary Art Museum, Ridgefield, Connecticut

Hypermental: Rampant Reality 1950–2000 from Salvador Dali to Jeff Koons, Kunsthaus Zurich, Zurich, Switzerland; traveled to: Hamburger Kunsthalle, Hamburg, Germany

Unnatural Science, Mass MoCA, North Adams, Massachusetts

Vision Machine, Musée des Beaux-Arts de Nantes, Nantes, France

Celebrating Modern Art: The Anderson Collection, San Francisco Museum of Modern Art, San Francisco, California

1999 *Mondo Immaginario—projektionen und pigmente,* Schendhalle, Zurich, Switzerland

Story, A/C Project Room, New York

Mario Diacono Gallery, Boston, Massachusetts

Hindsight—Recent Acquisitions and Gifts from the Permanent Collection, Whitney Museum of American Art, New York

Conceptual Art a Neurobiological Praxis, Thread Waxing Space, New York

Continued Investigation of the Relevance of Abstraction, Andrea Rosen Gallery, New York

1998 *Painting: Now and Forever, Part I,* Matthew Marks Gallery and Pat Hearn Gallery, New York

Parallel Worlds, Southeastern Center for Contemporary Art, Winston-Salem, North Carolina

Transatlantico, Centro Atlantico de Arte Moderno, Canary Islands, Spain

1997 *Map the Gap,* Storefront for Art and Architecture, New York

Art on Paper, Weatherspoon Art Gallery, University of North Carolina, Greensboro, North Carolina

Project Painting, Basilico Fine Arts and Lehmann Maupin, New York

In-form, Bravin Post Lee, New York

1997 Biennial Exhibition, Whitney Museum of American Art, New York

meteo-show, Galerie Meteo, Paris

1996 *New Work: Drawings Today,* San Francisco Museum of Modern Art, San Francisco, California

A Scattering Matrix, Richard Heller Gallery, Santa Monica, California

The Body of Painting, Mario Diacono Gallery, Boston, Massachusetts

Adicere Animos, La Galleria d'Arte Moderna e Contemporanea e Pinacoteca Nazionale, Cesena, Italy

AbFab, Feature, New York

Architecture/Application/Complication, Room, New York

Between the Acts, Ice Box, Athens, Greece

Between the Acts, c/o-Atle Gerhardsen, Oslo, Norway

Verrückt, Museum der Stadt, Arolsen, Germany

Screen, Friedrich Petzel Gallery, New York

1995 *Verrückt,* Schloss Agathenburg, Agathenburg, Germany

Summer Fling, Basilico Fine Arts, New York

A Vital Matrix, domestic setting gallery, Los Angeles, California

Möbius Strip, Basilico Fine Arts, New York

Ten + Ten, New York Studio School, New York

1994 *The Circumscribed Imagination on the Ruins of Tradition,* Mario Diacono Gallery, Boston, Massachusetts

Grey, Grodesky, Judd, Ritchie, Smithson, Mitchell Algus Gallery, New York

Matthew Ritchie, Nestor Otero, Leonora Vega Gallery, San Juan, Puerto Rico

1993 *Inconsequent,* Natalie Rivera, New York

New York, San Juan & Toronto, Leonora Vega, San Juan, Puerto Rico

Back Room, Natalie Rivera, New York

1992 *9 x 2* Installation Show, Artists Space, New York

Muranushi Lederman, New York

1991 *Blood,* JAARY, Finland

1990 *David McCaig & Matthew Ritchie,* Judy Nielsen Gallery, Chicago, Illinois

CHECKLIST OF THE EXHIBITION

CARROLL DUNHAM

Mesokingdom One, 2001
mixed media on linen, 80 x 64 inches (203.2 x 162.6 cm)
Collection of the artist

Shade, 2000–02
mixed media on linen, 80 x 74 inches (203.2 x 188 cm)
Collection of the artist

Mesokingdom Fourteen (Edge of Night), 2002
mixed media on linen, 96 x 93 inches (243.8 x 236.2 cm)
Collection of Terri and Phil Schrager, Omaha

Personal Distance (One), 2003
mixed media on linen, 70 x 77 inches (177.8 x 195.6 cm)
Collection of Lauren and Tim Schrager, Atlanta

Personal Distance (Two), 2003
mixed media on linen, 72 x 81 inches (182.9 x 205.7 cm)
Collection of Terri and Phil Schrager, Omaha

ELLEN GALLAGHER

Purgatorium, 2000
ink, pencil, plasticine, and paper on linen, 120 x 96 inches (304.8 x 243.8 cm)
Collection of the artist

ly, 2000
oil, ink, plasticine, and paper on linen, 72 x 84 inches (182.9 x 213.4 cm)
Purchased with funds from the Coffin Fine Arts Trust; Nathan Emory Coffin collection of the Des Moines Art Center, 2001.2

bling bling, 2001
enamel, rubber, and paper on linen, 96 x 120 inches (243.8 x 304.8 cm)
The Broad Art Foundation, Santa Monica

Psychoalphadiscobetabioaquadoloop, 2001
paper, cut rubber, and enamel on canvas, 96 x 120 inches (243.8 x 304.8 cm)
Collection of the artist

Watery Ecstatic (1 00 N, 7 00 E), 2003
cut paper, 60¼ x 74 inches (153 x 188 cm)
Collection of the artist; courtesy Gagosian Gallery

Watery Ecstatic (21 06 S, 53 36 E), 2003
cut paper, 60¼ x 74 inches (153 x 188 cm)
Collection of the artist; courtesy Gagosian Gallery

CHRIS OFILI

Monkey Magic—Sex, Money and Drugs, 1999
acrylic, collage, glitter, resin, pencil, map pins, and elephant dung on canvas, with two elephant dung supports,
96 x 72 inches (243.8 x 183 cm).
The Museum of Contemporary Art, Los Angeles, purchased with funds provided by the Broad Art Foundation

Dead Monkey—Sex, Money and Drugs, 2001
acrylic, oil, resin, map pins, and elephant dung on linen, with two elephant dung supports, 72 x 120 inches (183 x 304.8 cm)
Collection of Terri and Phil Schrager, Omaha; promised gift to Joslyn Art Museum

The Naked Spirit of Captain Shit and the Legend of the Black Stars, 2000
acrylic, collage, glitter, resin, map pins, and elephant dung on canvas, with two elephant dung supports, 96 x 72 inches (243.8 x 183 cm)
Collection of Ivelin and Craig Robins, Miami

Triple Beam Dreamer, 2001–02
acrylic, oil, leaves, glitter, polyester resin, map pins, and elephant dung on linen, with two elephant dung supports,
72 x 120 inches (182.9 x 304.8 cm)
Collection of Eileen Harris Norton, Santa Monica

NEO RAUCH

Neid, 1999
oil on canvas, 78 x 118 inches (200 x 299.8 cm)
Collection of Jay and Marsha Seeman, New York; courtesy David Zwirner, New York, and Galerie Eigen + Art, Berlin

Reflex, 2001
oil on canvas, 82 x 98 inches (210.2 x 250.2 cm)
Collection of Dianne Wallace, New York

Acker, 2002
oil on canvas, 82¾ x 98½ inches (210 x 250 cm)
Collection of Melva Bucksbaum and Raymond J. Learsy, New York

Schoepfer, 2002
oil on canvas, 84 x 100 inches (213.4 x 254 cm)
Private Collection, Marina Del Rey, California; courtesy David Zwirner, New York, and Galerie Eigen + Art, Berlin

Haus des Lehrers, 2003
oil on canvas, 100 x 80 inches (254 x 203.2 cm)
Collection of Susan and Michael Hort, New York

MATTHEW RITCHIE

Untitled Installation, Joslyn Art Museum, Omaha, January 31–April 25, 2004, incorporating:

Anti-City, 2000
oil and marker on canvas,
84 x 126 inches (213.4 x 320 cm)
The Speyer Family Collection, New York

Big Top, 2000
oil and marker on canvas,
84 x 96 inches (213.4 x 243.8 cm)
The Marc and Livia Straus Family Collection

Untitled, 2003
ink on denril, 12 x 48 inches (30.5 x 122 cm)
Courtesy the artist and Andrea Rosen Gallery, New York

Experienced Time, 2003
enamel on sintra, 86 x 312 inches (218 x 792 cm) (dimensions variable)
[not illustrated in catalogue]
Courtesy the artist and Andrea Rosen Gallery, New York

Coffin Weather, 2003
vinyl, 80 x 288 inches (203 x 731 cm) (dimensions variable)
[not illustrated in catalogue]
Courtesy the artist and Andrea Rosen Gallery, New York

ACKNOWLEDGMENTS

For this, my inaugural curatorial effort at Joslyn Art Museum, I am indebted to a number of my co-workers. The support and enthusiasm of our Director, J. Brooks Joyner, deftly set the stage, from beginning to end, for the presentation of this exhibition. Ruby C. Hagerbaumer's organizational skills, patience, and good humor proved crucial in the ongoing planning of the exhibition and catalogue. Penelope M. Smith I thank for her willingness and promptness in dealing with the loan agreements; Theodore W. James for his patience and skills in handling, shipping, and installing these paintings, some of which might have daunted a less stalwart teammate; and Janet L. Farber for her curatorial perspective and willingness to share her knowledge of the museum's workings with a neophyte.

Choosing the best possible works for an exhibition and actually securing their loan are two radically different undertakings. The latter of these two operations is often the most time-consuming curatorial function, one in which I fortunately had wonderful help and support. And, so, thanks to my colleagues, Chief Curator Paul Schimmel at the Museum of Contemporary Art in Los Angeles and Senior Curator Jeff Fleming at the Des Moines Art Center, for their help in securing an Ofili and a Gallagher loan respectively. I am thankful for the cheerful cooperation of Susan M. Taylor, Director of The Art Museum at Princeton University, and Joanne Heyler of The Broad Art Foundation, in securing crucial Gallagher paintings. The same collectors are very often over and over besieged by us curatorial types, and it is gratifying to know that they recognize their responsibility in sharing the pleasures of their acquisitions with the public. For this willingness I gratefully acknowledge the generosity of Melva Bucksbaum and Ray Learsy, Susan and Michael Hort, Eileen Harris Norton, Ivelin and Craig Robins, Phil and Terri Schrager, Tim and Lauren Schrager, Jay and Marsha Seeman, Jerry Speyer, Marc and Livia Straus, Dianne Wallace, and an anonymous collector. Various gallerists were not only critical in making contact with some of the private collectors not known to me personally but also in providing vital information on *Fabulism*'s artists. Most particularly helpful were Hanna Schouwink of the David Zwirner Gallery, Corinna Durland of Gavin Brown's enterprise, and Sarah Cohen of Andrea Rosen Gallery. Because of their frequent and direct contact with artists, such gallerists often achieve a deeper understanding of the artists' work than many a critic or curator. For their help in selecting their work to be shown here, and each in the lending of two works, I thank Carroll Dunham and Ellen Gallagher. Finally, I am endebted to Thomas Whitridge of Ink,Inc. for his excellent design and production of this catalogue.

My hope in curating is that the viewer will jubilate in beauty that provokes him or her into reflection, global and local. And, for myself, I have the same hope. Happily, I can report that my understanding of the work of all these artists grew still deeper as the exhibition's organization progressed. Carroll Dunham, who is the artist most familiar to me here, can still surprise me with his plane magic. Ellen Gallagher's enigmas began to expand, for me, figuratively as much as they have expanded literally. I never realized before just how joyous Matthew Ritchie's prodigal complexities could be. The more it confounds me the more the eloquence of Neo Rauch's muteness grows. And I got to catch a bigger glimpse of the profundities that lie beneath the super-seductive camouflage of Chris Ofili's brash beauty. Thank you all five for the still-growing bounty of your gifts.

KLAUS KERTESS

Adjunct Curator of Contemporary Art